Pelican Books
The Disintegrating West

Mary Kaldor was educated at Somerville College,
Oxford, where she read PPE. She worked from 1967 in
the Stockholm International Peace Research Institute
and became co-author of their major study *Arms
Trade with the Third World* (an abridged version of which
was published as a Pelican). In 1969 she joined the
Institute for the Study of International Organisations
in the University of Sussex, and in 1976 she moved
to the Science Policy Research Unit in the same
university. She was a Visiting Fellow at MIT in
1972–3 and a Visiting Fellow at the Otto Sur
Institute in the Free University of Berlin in 1974.
Her other publications include a number of articles
and a book entitled *European Defence Industries*:
National and International Implications, published by the
Institute for the Study of International Organisations,
University of Sussex. She is rapidly becoming
established as a leading critic on defence matters and
on international policy.

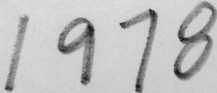

Mary Kaldor

The Disintegrating West

Penguin Books

To Julian

Penguin Books Ltd, Harmondsworth, Middlesex, England
Penguin Books, 625 Madison Avenue, New York, New York 10022,
U.S.A.
Penguin Books Australia Ltd, Ringwood, Victoria, Australia
Penguin Books Canada Ltd, 2801 John Street, Markham,
Ontario, Canada L3R 1B4
Penguin Books (N.Z.) Ltd, 182–190 Wairau Road, Auckland 10,
New Zealand

First published by Allen Lane 1978
Published in Pelican Books 1979

Made and printed in Great Britain by
Richard Clay (The Chaucer Press) Ltd, Bungay, Suffolk
Set in Monotype Garamond

Acknowledgements 7

Introduction 9

1   West versus West   14

2   East versus West   29

3   The Corporation and the State   47

4   Money   78

5   Trade   93

6   Oil   106

7   Defence   122

8   The Third World   150

9   Europe   173

10   Future Prospects   198

Index   209

Acknowledgements

This book could not have been written without the stimulus of discussion with my friends, colleagues, and relations. I am particularly grateful to Ulrich Albrecht, Alexander Cockburn, Stuart Holland, Brigadier Hunt, Brian Johnson, Nicholas Kaldor, Neil Middleton, Robin Murray, Julian Perry Robinson, Lino Pertile, Emma Rothschild, Robert Skidelsky, and Frances Stewart, who read and commented upon various versions of the manuscript. Needless to say, few, if any of them, agree with all the arguments.

I would also like to thank Jackie Fuschini, Gillian Joyce, Harriett Pertile, and Liz Woodhead for help in typing, and the Berghof Foundation for financial support while writing the book.

'I sometimes wonder what use there is in trying to protect the Western World against fancied external threats when the signs of disintegration within are so striking.'

George Kennan, *Encounter*, September 1976

Introduction

The sense of insecurity that is experienced unevenly in the West and associated in some way with the Soviet Union has waxed and waned over the last thirty years. The assumptions of détente are very different from the fears and anxieties of the cold war and different again from the pre-occupations of the immediate post-war period. Of late, some influential Westerners seem to be questioning those assumptions, in anticipation, perhaps, of yet another phase in international relationships.

This book tries to explain the new concern, and the shifts in opinion which preceded it, not in the changing mood of Soviet leaders, in geography or strategy, or even the interplay of capitalist and socialist relations but in the conflicts, based on real social needs, that are taking place within the West. Perceptions about external threats, while real enough as to their effect on action, are shaped as much by the situation of the perceiver as by the situation perceived. And the more remote the external threat, in terms of tangible economic and social connections, the greater is the domestic influence. This book is about the situation of the

West. Questions about the cold war or détente are subsidiary questions, following from those that arise out of the complex relationships between Western states and Western society. The conflict with the Soviet Union, which is described in Chapter 2, is viewed as a ritual, in which the ideologies of Soviet Marxism and White House liberalism mask the internal tensions of East and West. Failure to understand the nature of those tensions, to analyse and cope with the problems of the West, could have awful consequences, perhaps war.

In developing these arguments, the book adopts an alternative approach to the study of international relations. A conventional approach would treat the nation state as the independent actor in world affairs. In so far as it is possible to talk about an international system, it would be a relatively static system of competing nation states in which some states have greater bargaining power, expressed perhaps in numbers of soldiers or monetary reserves, than others. In this book, the nation state is treated as the momentary creation of history – being neither independent of society nor immutable. Indeed, a major theme is the passing of the nation state, or, rather, its struggle for survival in the face of increased interpenetration of Western societies and the dissipation of national constituencies. In particular, the multinational corporations are seen to play a key role in changing the rules of the international economy and upsetting the national balance of political forces.

Implicitly, this approach challenges the view that close links between nations, whether cultural or economic, lessen tension. Political conflict, that is to say, conflict between nation states, arises out of economic and social conflict – a process which is, of course, very complex, reflecting the complexity of the relationship between the state and society. Because the connections between closed systems, such as the United States and the Soviet Union, are so few, the conditions for economic and social conflict are unlikely to exist. Political conflict, therefore, in so far as it occurs, must be treated as the externalization of domestic conflict.

This approach can only be explored on the basis of an interpretation of the Western social system and the role of the nation state within it. This is sketchily and tentatively described in Chapter 3. The point is not to establish a theory, for this would be an immensely ambitious task, but to show how the assumptions made about the system manifest themselves in international relations, in economic disputes between nations (Chapters 4–6), in military policies (Chapter 7), and in political competition for spheres of influence (Chapter 8). In the chapter about Europe, the earlier abstract arguments are related to domestic political developments as well as international changes; this is because events that occur in Europe are the key to any prognosis about future international relations.

Apart from the chapter on defence, this book is not based on original research. Nor does it make much use of the conventional international relations literature. Rather, it draws heavily on the new and growing literature about the multinational corporation and about imperialism. A common theme in this literature is the imminence of change in the international system although there are many different views about the form it will take. Broadly, one can distinguish two schools of thought.[1] One, which can be found in the works of Harry Magdoff or Pierre Jalée, among others, would anticipate an extension of US domination, often referred to as 'super-imperialism', in which the main international conflict is that between the richest nations, led by the United States, and the poorest nations of the world. The second school of thought which is to be found largely in European literature, particularly the works of Robert Rowthorn and Ernest Mandel, would envisage the rise of what is known as 'inter-imperial

1. This controvesy is summarized by Robert Rowthorn in 'Imperialism in the 1970's – Unity or Rivalry' in Hugo Radice (ed.), *International Firms and Modern Imperialism*, Penguin Books, 1975 and in Ernest Mandel, *Late Capitalism*, New Left Books, 1975. They both mention a third school of thought, propounded by the Hungarian economist Varga, known as Ultra-Imperialism, in which Europe and Japan break American hegemony and share the leadership of the capitalist world.

rivalry', the increased power of Japan and Europe and a growing conflict between these nations and the United States; the political or territorial struggle for the Third World is the consequence of this rivalry. This book is in the European tradition. It does not exclude the prospect of renewed American hegemony but it would argue that this is conditioned by the rivalry with Europe and Japan rather than the suppression of revolt in the Third World *per se*.

The book, however, is confined to rivalry within the West. It does not deal with Asia and this may prove to be a major weakness; it was necessary to impose some limits on the scope of what is a very large and almost all-embracing subject. It may be that the relationship between the United States, Western Europe and the Soviet Union is paralleled by a similar relationship between the United States, Japan and China in the East, or it may be that a study of Asia would produce quite different conclusions. China and Japan are apparently less powerful than the Soviet Union or a future Western Europe; on the other hand, the dynamism of Asian societies may result in changes that engulf the kind of developments in the West that are described here.

Such speculation is part of the more general anticipation of a new division of the world into super nation states, a new global constellation of continental groupings as was predicted by several important thinkers in the late nineteenth century,[1] by such writers as George Orwell and by a number of recent political leaders – the Chinese talk about the 'five-pronged star' and the former President Nixon used the more prosaic term 'multipolarity'. Perhaps it is too soon to develop a language; the immediate and important issues are about the process of creation – a process, like earlier global changes, that is likely to involve terrible convulsive destruction. In a sense, this is the book of a political doomster. But it is not entirely without hope. Expectations of doom, such as those about ecocide and food scarcity, tend to be based on conservative assump-

1. For a description of these, see Geoffrey Barraclough, *An Introduction to Contemporary History*, Penguin Books, 1967.

tions. It is to be hoped that the assumptions will be disproved and that radical social change can provide the opportunity for a different kind of world – one perhaps that is not based on nations and super nations.

1   West versus West

The pundits of the international order are predicting the decline of American authority. 'The most lasting consequences of Vietnam', according to the late Professor Buchan, 'may well be on Americans' perceptions of themselves, of the world, and of the proper role of the United States in it.' For Vietnam 'happened to coincide with the emergence of a number of endemic domestic problems and a loss of American strategic and economic predominance'.[1] The changing role of America is presaged in the declining rate of economic growth (the American citizen is no longer the richest in the world) and in the apparent break-up of the liberal world economy (the crises about oil, money and food). It has involved the fragmentation of political power – the rise of Europe, Japan and oil-rich Arabia, the successful revolutions in Indo-China and Southern Africa. And it could result in a new uncertain international order, with new forms of political confrontation, whose dimensions

1. Alastair Buchan, 'The Indochina War and World Politics', *Foreign Affairs*, vol. 53, no. 4, July 1975.

are impossible to calculate. Can we interpret these developments and understand by them more than the chance concurrence of events? Is there some common plot with a limited number of endings? One way to look for it is to start with the changing basis of American authority and to see how this delineates the possible range of international activities. It is a widely shared conviction, popularized by such Presidents as Woodrow Wilson and Lyndon Johnson, that the basis of liberty, in whose name American authority is exercised, is the free enterprise system, i.e. capitalism. One might begin with this conviction and, from such a perspective, sketch a view of American post-war foreign policy.

Perhaps the most obvious feature of the capitalist system, over which America presides, is its unprecedented accumulation of material wealth. But it would be quite wrong to suppose that this has been achieved without cost; neither the efforts that went into it nor the benefits that came out of it have been distributed evenly. On the contrary, capitalist growth is, by its very nature, an uneven process. It proceeds through the rise and fall of technologies, corporations, industrial sectors, nations and even continents. It depends on the concentration of resources in the hands of the most efficient enterprises, located in the most advantageous regions. It is a Darwinian process, which might be termed 'survival of the fastest'; unprofitable slow-growing firms are eliminated, high cost slow-growing regions stagnate, experiencing unemployment and low standards of living.

The financial and physical concentration of resources, and hence continued growth, depends on an unfettered world economy, on the free movement of capital, labour and goods. This has to be guaranteed by a strong state. Otherwise the governments of slow-growing regions might interfere with the transfer of resources to fast-growing regions and attempt to obtain a larger share of the world's product through tariffs and physical restrictions of various kinds. This would slow down world economic growth, provoke competitive responses from the governments of fast-growing regions, and eventually push the world into economic crisis.

In the mid-nineteenth century, Britain acted as the guarantor of the liberal world economy. The City could provide loans to governments in need; the loans were spent on British goods because Britain was the most advanced and fast-growing nation. The government could send gunboats against those who protested because the British navy was pre-eminent. A number of American historians (e.g. William Appleman Williams and C. Lloyd Gardner) have argued that since the 1890s, with the decline of Britain and the emergence of the New Mercantilism of the European empires, the beginnings of America's own international expansion and the enunciation of the 'Open Door' principle, America's foreign policy has been conditioned by the need to prevent the competition between economic blocs. Because of the dynamism of the American economy, because America was the fastest-growing region, this kind of foreign policy could expect to gather support from labour and farmers as well as successful industrialists. Certainly, Roosevelt's New Dealers were convinced by the economic nationalism of the 1930s and the warfare between sterling, dollars, marks and yen, that after the Second World War the United States must take over Britain's historic role. A week after Japan surrendered, the Secretary of State, James F. Byrnes, made a speech in which he said: 'Our international and our domestic policies are inseparable. Our foreign relations inevitably affect employment in the United States. Prosperity and depression in the United States just as inevitably affect our relations with the other nations of the world.' He expressed a

firm conviction that a durable peace cannot be built on an economic foundation of exclusive blocs . . . and economic warfare . . . [A liberal trading system] imposes special responsibilities upon those who occupy a dominant position in world trade. Such is the position of the United States . . . In many countries throughout the world our political and economic creed is in conflict with ideologies which reject both of these principles. To the extent that we are able to manage our domestic affairs successfully we shall win converts to our creed in every land.[1]

While the New Dealers failed in their attempt to dismantle war-time economic barriers and to pursue a friendly economic competition with the Soviet Union, it can be argued that the policies of the Truman Administration which laid the groundwork for all later Administrations were based on the same premises, i.e. the suppression of competitive economic blocs and the supremacy of America within the capitalist system. The economic concessions offered to those countries where social upheaval threatened their membership in the capitalist system merely served to improve America's economic position. Both the Marshall Plan and the aid programmes to underdeveloped countries that came after it were enthusiastically welcomed by American exporters. At the same time, the system of military alliances, ostensibly directed against the Soviet Union, provided a formal basis for American authority.

The argument that the Soviet threat was both exaggerated and known to be exaggerated by the post-war American leaders has been admirably documented by a number of revisionist historians of the cold war.[2] In March 1949, before the creation of NATO, John Foster Dulles declared that: 'I do not know any responsible official, military or civilian, in this Government or any Government who believes that the Soviet Government now plans conquest by open military means.'[3] And his statement

1. Quoted in Walter Lafeber, *America, Russia and the Cold War, 1945–71*, John Wiley & Sons, Inc., New York, 1972, p. 7.

2. See, for example, David Horowitz, *From Yalta to Vietnam*, Penguin Books, 1967; William Appleman Williams, *The Tragedy of American Diplomacy*, Delta Books, New York, 1962; Gar Alperovitz, *Atomic Diplomacy: Hiroshima and Potsdam*, Martin Secker & Warburg, 1965; Denna Frank Fleming, *The Cold War and Its Origins, 1917–1920*, Allen & Unwin, 1961.

3. Quoted in Horowitz, op. cit., p. 80.

was corroborated by the Secretary of Defense, James V. Forrestal, by the US ambassador to the Soviet Union, by George Kennan who was then Chairman of the Policy planning staff at the State Department as well as others.[1] During the Congressional Hearings about the creation of NATO, it was made clear that the military significance of NATO was minor; the military strength of the West was thought to reside in America's monopoly of atomic power and there were no proposals to augment conventional manpower in Europe. It has been suggested that its main purpose was to prevent the emergence of an independent power bloc,[2] through ensuring the permanent division of Europe. Harriman said that, without NATO, there 'would be a reorientation' and 'a restrengthening of those who believe in appeasement and neutrality'. Acheson said that: 'Unity in Europe requires the continuing association and support of the United States. Without it, free Europe would split apart.'[3]

The subsequent military assistance programme, the establishment of an integrated command system, and the rearmament of West Germany can also be interpreted in a similar fashion. The division of Germany ensured the defeat of the Social Democrats who favoured a united neutral Germany. The military assistance and integrated command system brought the impeccable newly created Bundeswehr together with the armies of Italy and France under the supreme command of an American, and undermined the 'third force' (between the United States and the Soviet Union) ideology that was currently popular in Italy and France. Both Dulles and Eisenhower emphasized the key role of West Germany in a new revitalized Western Europe within the Atlantic System.[4]

1. ibid.
2. Lafeber, op. cit.
3. Quoted, ibid., p. 78.
4. See William C. Cromwell, 'The United States', and Josef Joffe, 'Germany and the Atlantic Alliance. The Politics of Dependence, 1961–68' in William C. Cromwell (ed.), *Political Problems of Atlantic Partnership: National Perspectives*, College of Europe Studies in Contemporary European Issues, 3, Bruges, 1969.

Concern about the emergence of independent power blocs can be said to have prompted the new American interest in underdeveloped countries towards the end of the 1950s and Kennedy's response to the creation of the European Common Market[1] and the rise of Gaullism. Kennedy's 'Grand Design' for Europe, put forward in his 'Declaration of Interdependence' in 1962, encompassed plans for the sharing of nuclear forces and increased trade liberalization. The former was designed, in McNamara's words, to 'avoid the fragmentation and compartmentalization of NATO nuclear power which would be dangerous to all of us',[2] while the latter was an attempt to reduce the specifically European character of the Common Market, with the aid of British membership.[3] When de Gaulle vetoed British membership he expressed his concern that Europe would 'in the last resort emerge as a colossal Atlantic Community, dependent upon and controlled by the United States'.[4]

Already, by that time, the American rate of economic growth had slowed down and a balance of payments deficit had appeared. The traditional belief that trade liberalization would improve the balance of payments was one of the motives behind Kennedy's 'Declaration of Interdependence'. But it was not until the middle 1960s

1. In 1958, the six nations – France, Italy, West Germany and Benelux – which had created the European Coal and Steel Community in 1950 went on to create the European Economic Community (the Common Market) comprising a tariff-free zone, a common external tariff, and a common agricultural policy.

2. Quoted in Cromwell, op. cit., p. 82. American spokesmen made it clear that shared nuclear forces were not necessary from a 'strictly military viewpoint', and that 'the consent of the United States would have to be obtained prior to the firing of any of the nuclear weapons jointly owned and controlled by the participating nations'. Further, the nuclear weapons assigned to joint control would only have amounted to 5 per cent of the total nuclear striking force.

3. In the Trade Expansion Act of 1962, Kennedy proposed a device which would have involved the creation of an Atlantic Common Market, had Britain joined in 1963 (see Chapter 5).

4. Quoted in F. Roy Willis, *France, Germany and the New Europe, 1947–67*, Stanford University Press, California, 1968, p. 303.

that the effects of a faltering economy were experienced by important sections of society, undermining the consensus behind American foreign policy. And it was not until 1971 that new domestic pressures began to introduce a new element of parochialism into America's world role.

From the 1950s, the direction of uneven development underwent an historic reversal.[1] America lost its pre-eminent position as the fastest-growing region in the world and was overtaken by Japan, on the one hand, and, on the other, by that part of Western Europe that is known as Lotharingia – that part, comprising West Germany, Bene-lux, north-east France and northern Italy, which Charle-magne placed under the command of his second son Lothar.[2] American capital, the big multinational corpor-ations, began to invest in those regions. Indeed, the heyday of the multinationals can be said to date from this period. American consumers began to buy cars, televisions or calculators produced in Japan and Lotharingia. Likewise, domestic American producers began to import machines and steel. From the middle 1960s, the rate of productivity growth failed to keep up with the rate of growth of money wages, and this, combined with the Vietnam war spending and monopoly pricing by big multinational corporations, led to an accelerating rate of inflation. Organized labour were among the first to protest, arguing that the export of capital and the import of goods represented the loss of thousands of jobs and that inflation was eroding the real income of industrial workers. A spokesman for the AFL–CIO (American organized labour) told the Senate Finance Committee that the US was 'becoming a nation of hamburger stands . . . a country stripped of industrial capacity and meaningful work . . . a service economy . . . a nation of citizens busily buying and selling cheese-burgers and root beer floats'.[3] Workers were joined by

1. The reasons for the reversal are discussed in Chapter 3.
2. The term was first used by R. Perroux.
3. Quoted in Richard J. Barnet and Ronald E. Müller, *Global Reach: The Power of the Multinational Corporations*, Jonathan Cape, 1974, p. 306.

domestic producers in sectors such as textiles, dairy products, steel and leather and by some sections of international business such as oil or arms threatened by foreign
competition.

In 1971, the first trade deficit made its appearance
and, subsequently, the Administration took – or allowed to
be taken – a series of measures that amounted to a parochial
policy. The elements of this policy were the devaluation of
the dollar, the rise in the price of food and oil, the reduction in official aid, both economic and military, the promo-
tion of arms sales, and the withdrawal of American troops
stationed abroad. They led to an improvement in the
American balance of payments, a recovery – possibly
temporary – in the American economy, a slowing down of
world economic growth and a series of political crises in
foreign countries.

It cannot be said that this policy was consciously
formulated. On the contrary, the concepts and conceptual-
izers of American foreign policy remain those that grew up
in the cold war period. The language of diplomacy is still
the language of international liberalism despite the fact
that America is no longer the guarantor of the liberal world
order and that America's international authority is being
used to impose new barriers to the free flow of resources.
Rather, this new shift in American foreign policy was the
piecemeal response to a variety of special interests affected
by the decline of the American economy. Thus, for example, farmers, hit by recession and inflation, pressed for a
change in US farm policy which involved the dismantling
of grain reserves, the ending of food aid and the rapid rise
in world food prices.[1] As we shall see, a similar process was
taking place in such spheres as oil and arms. In so far as
there existed an overall response to American decline, it
was a response to the financial problems of power, conceived in terms of the balance of payments difficulties. The
balance of payments could be treated as a kind of company

1. See Emma Rothschild, 'Food Politics', *Foreign Affairs*,
January 1976.

statement, the profit and loss account of America Inc. The well-being of the dollar is a signal or symptom of the state of the American economy and the return on international political transactions such as military spending or aid. The fact is that even without domestic pressures on the government the basis for America's international authority was weakening and this was being increasingly recognized abroad.

The trend to parochialism is by no means irreversible. It is opposed not only by the makers of American foreign policy who have not yet adjusted to the new conditions of the world but also by the most powerful sections of American society, the international business community. While labourers in the automobile or electronics industry might demand restrictions on imported goods, their bosses are busily making profits out of the dynamism of the German and Japanese economies. It can be argued that, in the early 1970s, the government was ill-prepared for the onslaught of parochial interests. Now, with the recovery of the economy and the winding-up of the Vietnam war, it is possible to reassert America's world role. The increase in military spending, the appeal for greater standardization and integration in NATO, the renewed efforts to create international institutions to cope with money, energy and food, can all be interpreted as a resumption of international authority. In other words, American foreign policy is poised in two directions: on the one hand, a parochial tendency, supported by labour and domestic producers, which would give priority to the domestic economy and, on the other hand, an internationalist stance, favoured by the multinational corporations which put the world economy before the domestic economy. Both directions would have important but different international consequences.

A parochial policy could eventually lead to the break-up of the liberal world economy and the rise of new centres of power, pursuing competitive economic policies. The most important of these would be the nascent European Community. The movement for European unity has always been supported by big business, both European and American, which favours the creation of large unified markets. It is joined by other sections of society located in the fastest-growing regions of Europe – the Lotharingian belt. This group, known as 'the Atlanticists', sees the European Community as the first step towards the creation of an Atlantic Community, a move towards the realization of the New Dealers' conception of the world, the Utopia of a multinational corporation, a unified world market with a single capitalist state.

      There is another Europeanist group, however, which one might term Gaullist. This group comprises national producers – farmers, arms manufacturers and oil companies, for example – threatened by American competition, together with ruling politicians in the slow-growing regions of Europe who can no longer settle the conflict between the internationalist demands of big business and domestic economic requirements. This group, which has many adherents within the Community bureaucracy, is responsible for the external tariff, the agricultural policy, for European as opposed to Atlantic collaboration on arms and other high technology projects, and the efforts to pursue independent policies towards the Soviet Union and the Third World. Whereas the first group, the Atlanticists, might derive its ideology from mid-nineteenth-century liberalism and take as its heroes the liberators of Italy, Mazzini and Garibaldi, the second group has more in common with the New Mercantilism of late nineteenth-century Europe, the idea of empire based on economic necessity. De Gaulle's views have much in common with those of the German economic historian, Gustav Schmoller, who realized that 'the course of the twentieth century will be determined by the competition between the Russian, English, American, and perhaps the Chinese world empires, and by their aspirations to reduce all the other smaller states to dependence on them' and who saw 'in a central European customs federation the nucleus of something which may save from destruction not only the political independence of those states, but Europe's higher ancient culture itself'.[1] Despite the imperial vision, the members of the Gaullist group might be regarded as the parochial Europeans.

The cost of American recovery was not borne by Lotharingia or, for that matter, Japan. Increased American income was spent, at least in part, on German cars and machines, Japanese televisions and so on. Oil revenues were exchanged for manufactured goods produced in Lotharingia and for Deutschmarks. The people who paid for the higher cost of food, oil, arms and loans to mitigate their difficulties, who experienced the worst combination of inflation and unemployment, were located in the peripheral regions of Europe and in the underdeveloped world. In Europe, their protests were expressed in new radical nationalistic tendencies, in the strengthening of the Communist parties in France and Italy, in the rise of new regional parties, such as Scottish and Breton Nationalists.

Unlike America, the smaller nation state – Britain, France or Italy – has little power with which to carry out effective parochial economic policies. In particular, the enormous growth in the size of individual capitalist units, i.e. the multinational corporation, has eroded most of the conventional instruments of economic policy. Faced with a disintegrating consensus, a favoured solution is dissolution, membership in a new European state where local and apparently particular protest would be overwhelmed and where certain parochial interests – farmers and arms companies – can perhaps receive better protection. Hence, the increase in Gaullist-type pressure for European unity. The alternative (and it is a real alternative) is more political struggle, violence and even revolution – a disintegrating crisis-ridden Europe.

Thus America's parochialism has strengthened parochial elements in Europe and intensified the contradictory trends towards integration and disintegration. And these effects are not confined to Europe. Similar struggles have emerged in underdeveloped countries. With the end

1. Quoted in Fritz Fischer, *Germany's Aims in the First World War*, Chatto & Windus, 1967, p. 4.

of aid and the rise in the cost of imports, nation states, caught in the agony of repression and revolution, famine and war, have attempted to improve their bargaining power by reducing dependence on the United States and exploiting the competition between Europe, Japan and America. Uneven development is hierarchical. Fast-growing regions exploit slow-growing regions. Slow-growing regions exploit slower-growing regions. Just as the American recovery was paid for by the poorest people, so the weaker European producers see the underdeveloped world as a market for arms and non-competitive manufacturers and a source for cheaper raw materials. In so far as governments in the Third World – Peru, perhaps, or Pakistan, not to mention the Arab countries – need wider political support for independent policies, they too can enhance Gaullist pressures for a Super Europe.

So it was in the early 1970s that the European Community was enlarged by the membership of Britain, Ireland and Denmark and that a number of important disputes with the United States emerged. It was at the height of the oil crisis of 1973–4 that Kissinger was able to say that

> the biggest problem American foreign policy confronts right now is not to regulate competition with its enemies . . . but how to bring our friends to a realisation that there are greater common interests than simply self-assertiveness and that the seeming victory they are striving for is going to prove hollow in an atmosphere of constant strife and endless competition.[1]

Kissinger was restating the traditional American phobia for competitive economic blocs and, subsequently, other American leaders reiterated the traditional American argument that Kennedy put to de Gaulle in 1963 that unity is necessary 'to hold back the expansion of communism . . . Acting alone, neither the United States nor Europe could be certain of success or survival. The reality of purposes, therefore, is that which serves to unite us is right and what

1. *The Times*, 12 March 1974.

tends to divide us is wrong . . .'[1] Indeed it is interesting to note that Kissinger's opposition to Communist participation in the Italian government is not based on the evils of communism *per se* but on the concern that this will

> produce governments in which the degree of cooperation that has become characteristic of Atlantic relations will become increasingly difficult, in which their own internal priorities are going to be away from concern with defense, which will produce new opportunities for outside pressures and a move towards a more neutralist conception of foreign policy.[2]

In other words, he was concerned that a stronger Italian Communist party might promote an independent European bloc.

The new emphasis on the common defence, the expressed anxiety about Soviet naval expansion and the new 'dollar' gap,[3] the appeal for greater integration and standardization of NATO military forces are, in effect, the traditional tools for holding the West together. Similarly, the international arrangements proposed for the regulation of money, energy and food are little more than the traditional American economic concessions in a new international guise. If they are to be effective, they must be largely financed and organized by the United States.[4]

1. Quoted in Horowitz, *From Yalta to Vietnam*, p. 387.
2. *International Herald Tribune*, 15 April 1976.
3. The CIA has adopted a new method for calculating the dollar equivalent of Soviet military spending, and, using this method, it claims to show that the Soviet Union spends more on defence than does the United States. Congressman Les Aspin has shown that using the same method to calculate the rouble equivalent of American military spending the opposite conclusion is reached.
4. It is possible, of course, that in a Super Europe, Atlanticist elements would prevail and offer economic concessions to the United States. But such a scenario is inherently unstable. For such economic concessions are equivalent to American parochialism, strengthening parochial elements in Europe and imposing the same dilemmas on a Super European government as are faced by the current US Administration. If, as some economists suggest, the changing pattern of economic growth is accompanied by a secular decline in the

Unlike the immediate post-war period, however, this international posture will not benefit the American economy. Overseas spending in the form of aid and foreign military intervention will not return to the United States through the purchase of American goods and services. Some sections of the community, high finance and big business, may benefit from debt repayments and profit repatriation, but in general the additional international resources will follow the orthodox capitalist pattern and concentrate on the fastest-growing regions, Lotharingia and Japan. The result will be a new trade deficit and re-newed domestic problems. As the cost of being inter-nationalist rises, it is possible to envisage an increasing resort to military, as opposed to economic, instruments of power, to repression both at home and abroad and exagger-ated emphasis on military alliances through ritual hostility towards the Soviet Union.

This is the unpalatable dilemma that American policy-makers face. On the one hand, a parochial policy designed to support the American economy, at the expense of deepening social conflict abroad slowing down world economic growth, and the likely emergence of new centres of power, particularly in Europe, able to conduct competi-tive economic policies in precisely the manner that post-war American policy was designed to avoid. On the other hand, a renewed attempt at international authority revers-ing the recovery of the American economy, exacerbating domestic conflict, and undermining the very basis of international authority.

In practice, of course, the choice is not so clear. Policy is likely to veer from one to the other and back again, according to the economic exigencies of the moment and the changing constellation of political forces. And these shifts of policy will correspond to shifts in the focus of international conflict; on the one hand, West versus West

global rate of economic growth, then economic concessions of this kind are likely to be viewed as sacrifice rather than munificence and the constraints on a government that demands such sacrifice will be correspondingly greater.

exacerbating North versus South and on the other hand, West versus East – the latter conditioned by the former. And unless there is some fundamental social change in which the principle of 'survival of the fastest' is abandoned, this cycle of rivalry within the West followed by hostility towards the East can do little else than degenerate into unbearable tension.

2 East versus West

There is, of course, another more orthodox interpretation of America's post-war foreign policy. It holds that the Soviet Union and communism, which it represents just as America represents the forces striving for liberty, is a fundamentally expansionist and aggressive power. American leaders have set out to do exactly what they claim, defend the West against this totalitarian threat. Détente has been made possible by a modification in the attitude of Soviet leaders and by the effective deterrent of the balance of terror. But Atlantic rivalry, by weakening the West, by 'sapping the impulse for a common defence',[1] to use Kissinger's phrase, could rekindle Soviet ambitions.

The difficulty with this view is that it is based on a failure to analyse the Soviet system, on a kind of bad guy/good guy conception of international politics. It can be argued that any attempt to identify the real interests of the Soviet state, as opposed to the ideological predilections of particular leaders, would show that these are not so much competitive as complementary with the interests of the United States. Politically, a case can be made that both

1. Atlantic Charter, April 1973.

sides need the excuse of the other for holding together respective spheres of influence[1] and for justifying a military momentum which has more to do with domestic political exigencies than with external strategic requirements. Economically, the United States is much more advanced than the Soviet Union and the two countries do not compete for the same markets and the same raw materials. On the contrary, the Soviet Union needs Western technology and, recently, American grain, while the United States and Europe need Soviet markets and some of the Soviet raw materials.

Détente could be said to institutionalize this relationship. It is a kind of guarantee of mutual non-interference, and a way of avoiding the risks of ideological hostility. Indeed, this is enshrined in the Basic Principles of Détente, agreed on by the American and Soviet leaders in 1972, which stipulate that nations must

Prevent the development of situations capable of causing a dangerous exacerbation of their relations.
Do their utmost to avoid military confrontation.
Recognize that efforts to obtain unilateral advantages at the expense of the other, directly or indirectly, are inconsistent with these objectives. . . .[2]

Détente also provides the conditions for 'controlling' the arms race, that is to say, for agreements which channel the arms race in mutually advantageous directions and lessen its most dangerous risks. It also allows for increased economic and scientific exchange.

We have already indicated, albeit sketchily, how the American need for an external enemy – as well as markets – can be explained with reference to the Western social system. A similar explanation might be put forward

1. This was the essence of the remarks made by Helmut Sonnenfeldt, one of Kissinger's aides, to US ambassadors in Europe in March 1976 when he described the relation between the Soviet Union and the rest of East Europe as 'organic'. These remarks became subject to heavy criticism.
2. *Department of State Bulletin*, 26 June 1972.

for Soviet foreign policy. Just as it is wrong to accept the statements of American leaders at their face value – to suppose, for example, that Nixon's concept of liberty truly reflects the ideals of the American revolution – so it would be a mistake to view the Soviet regime, as it is viewed by apologists as well as its bitterest Western enemies, as a socialist state irrevocably committed to world revolution and to suppose that Soviet Marxism is no different from Bolshevism. But it would be nearly as wrong to treat the Soviet state as a capitalist state, tending towards the West, on account of its 'technostructure', as Galbraith and others would put it, or on account of bureaucratic and international competition, along the lines of a Trotskyist analysis. There is a fundamental difference between the Soviet system and the capitalist system and that is the fact that the Soviet system as yet is not subject to the same compulsion to expand, although the leadership may have particular expansionist ambitions. Under a capitalist system, individual enterprises must expand or face bankruptcy. Similarly, regions that fail to grow face severe economic difficulties. In the Soviet Union, bureaucrats may be penalized for not reaching paper targets or following instructions correctly but the system of planning prevents the elimination of inefficient enterprises – indeed, by law workers cannot be dismissed – and can cope with particular regional problems. Even the competition with the West cannot be said to necessitate expansion; the Soviet Union has certain military and economic requirements for survival but these are not necessarily subject to perpetual growth. Even if the worst American intentions were assumed, it is not necessary to match the West gun for gun and missile for missile. For one thing, much of the West's armoury is superfluous, a massive overkill capacity, for example, or certain large weapon platforms like aircraft carriers rendered obsolescent by new missile technologies.[1] For another, the requirements of defence are less than those of

1. See, for example, Enthoven and Wayne Smith, *How Much is Enough?*, Harper & Row, New York, 1971.

offence. To some extent, this has been recognized by the Soviet Union in the emphasis on submarine defence instead of expensive surface ships and in Khrushchev's idea – never fulfilled – of a 'new look' strategy based on new missile technologies. In so far as the Soviet Union has aimed at 'parity', and has also acquired superfluous weaponry, this should be construed neither as a response to American activity nor as evidence of Soviet expansionism. Apart from recent troop increases specifically allocated to the control of the Socialist bloc – garrison troops in Eastern Europe or the border war with China – military decision-making bears little definite relation to external strategic events. Rather, the Soviet arms build-up must be seen as the consequence of an internal industrial and military momentum – over-capacity in heavy industry and a powerful military interest group thrown up by certain inherent features of the Soviet system, as we shall see below. The point is that the militarists and the ideologists of the Soviet Union may pursue expansionary policies but, unlike their Western counterparts, they do not for the moment have to; they can still afford to retreat.

The Soviet system was shaped by the historical conditions in which it emerged from the civil war in the early 1920s. Far from being part of a wider socialist system created by revolutions in central Europe as the Bolsheviks had anticipated, the new Soviet state was politically isolated in an economically backward environment. Out of this situation, two critical features of the Soviet system emerged. The first was the decision, based on the assumption that socialism can only be achieved in an advanced capitalist economy, to put industrialization before socialization, to sacrifice the needs of the individual to the rapid creation of heavy industry, under the control of the state instead of the people. The second was the fact that to carry out this policy of industrialization, the Bolshevik leaders were dependent on the old Czarist bureaucracy. Lenin told the 4th Congress of the Comintern in 1922:

We took over the old machinery of state and that

was our misfortune . . . We have a vast army of government employees, but lack the educated forces to exercise real control over them . . . At the top we have, I don't know how many, but at all events no more than a few thousand . . . Down below there are hundreds of thousands of old officials we got from the Czar and from bourgeois society . . .[1]

In the political struggles between different factions of the Bolshevik party, it was inevitable that the victors, i.e. Stalin and Zinoviev, should make use of these lower level bureaucrats, and that these same bureaucrats should come to constitute a new privileged class.

The system which thus emerged was one in which the state itself constituted the ruling class, in the sense that it controlled production and distribution as well as the political domain. Its *raison d'être* was industrialization, and industrialization under the control of the state became a ruling principle of the society, reflected in the internal structure of the state. The pre-eminence of the state did not mean that it could be used as the personal instrument of a particular leader as some would explain the worst excesses of Stalin. Within the bureaucratic structure is likely to be found the same kind of pluralistic competition for power that characterizes politics both inside and outside the structure of Western government. Just as in the West no single group can monopolize power – although obviously some groups have more influence than others – without undermining the stability of society, and various devices, such as the electoral system, prevent this from occurring, so in the Soviet Union the system operates through compromise. According to Herbert Marcuse the devices which prevent effective control by one faction of the bureaucracy are:

On the one side, the central plan, in spite of all its vagaries, loopholes, and corrections, ultimately supersedes and integrates the special interests; on the other side, the entire bureaucracy, up to the highest level, is subject

1. V. I. Lenin, *Collected Works*, vol. 33, Moscow, 1965, p. 430.

to the competitive terror, or, after the relaxation of the terror, to the highly incalculable application of political or punitive measures, leading to the loss of power.[1]

In this way, the overall interest of the Soviet state, which is linked to industrialization, as opposed to particular sectional interests, can become the overriding characteristic of the Soviet system. Just as Western leaders have come to identify political and intellectual freedom with the survival of the free enterprise system, so Soviet leaders have 'trans-substantiated', to use Marcuse's term, class struggle into the political interests of their state and have identified the future of socialism with the survival of the Soviet system. Hence the term 'proletarian internationalism' to characterize the ideology of Moscow's hegemony.

This system gives rise to two main requirements which condition relations with the rest of the world. One is the need for Western technology. In the first two five-year plans, 1928–37, imports from the West paid for with raw materials and gold, played a key role, as did war-time lend-lease programmes in later plans.[2] Since the late 1950s, the need for Western technology has received even greater emphasis. This is because the Soviet Union has been unable to achieve the rapid rates of growth of the early period of industrialization. Unlike the United States, this failure to grow is not due to lack of investment. Fixed capital formation as a proportion of GNP (Gross National Product) is around twice the proportion that prevails in most Western industrial countries and yet the rate of growth is roughly the same. The difference has to be explained by low productivity and surplus capacity. This stems from two main causes. First, the rigidity of the system, the lack of individual initiative, and the emphasis on the fulfilment of formal instructions. Managers are more concerned about

1. Herbert Marcuse, *Soviet Marxism, A Critical Analysis*, Penguin Books, 1971, p. 94.

2. For a detailed description of Soviet dependence on Western technology, see Antony C. Sutton, *Western Technology and Soviet Economic Development, 1917–1930*, Stanford University Press, Stanford, California, 1968.

quantity than quality; they have to meet numerical production targets. Innovation would disrupt those targets. Workers are alienated, doing tedious jobs, subject neither to punishment nor reward. They cannot be dismissed; they are not eligible for many consumption goods produced for the privileged class of bureaucrats and sold in special shops; nor, would it seem, do they have an ideological satisfaction in the system. Because statistics may often be juggled upwards for the sake of an individual career and because the planners invariably make mistakes, over-optimistic plans are made, leading to over-investment; shortages and bottlenecks become endemic, slowing down work, encouraging hoarding and exacerbating the problem of surplus capacity. One Soviet economist has estimated that waste absorbs 30–50 per cent of total production.[1]

A second cause of the low productivity growth is the over-emphasis on heavy industry and on arms. Precisely because these were the industries which received priority in the first five-year plans, they have acquired an internal momentum which is very difficult to check. Under capitalism, investment decisions are taken by individual entrepreneurs and mistakes are ultimately penalized by bankruptcy. Crises provide the mechanism for shifting resources from inefficient declining sectors to new dynamic sectors. In the Soviet system, investment decisions are largely the product of bargaining between different sections of the bureaucracy. It is inevitable that the most powerful groups, even if they represent the least dynamic industrial sectors, claim the largest share of the investment fund. It can be argued that these industries have reached a stage, which all industries reach sooner or later, where further technical improvements are difficult to achieve and further additions to output have little contribution to make to the future growth of the economy. A particular concern of Soviet economists is with the need to shift from extensive to intensive industrialization; by this, they mean the shift from industrial growth achieved through the expansion of

1. See H. Ticktin, 'Towards a Political Economy of the USSR', *Critique no. 1*, Spring 1973.

the workforce and the absorption of surplus agricultural population (which is rapidly diminishing) and growth achieved through the adoption of new techniques. Yet the latter is inhibited by the priority given to traditional industries. Thus, in 1970, Sakharov sent a letter to the Soviet leaders, together with the historian Roy Medvedev and the physicist Turchin, in which they wrote:

> The gulf between the United States and us is all the greater in the newest and most revolutionary sectors of the economy. We are ahead of America in coal extraction, but behind in oil, gas and electric energy; we are ten years behind in chemicals and infinitely behind in computer technology . . . We simply live in another era.[1]

In the mid 1960s, economic reforms, aimed at increasing individual initiative through decentralization and material incentives, were introduced. But they have not proved very effective. Decentralization has been undermined by the need to acquire centrally distributed investment funds. Further, in so far as it has been successful, it has tended to increase sectional interests. The defence industries group, for example, has increased its influence over military decision-making; it can be argued that the appointment of Ustinov, former head of the defence industries group, to the post of Minister of Defence indicates less civilian control over the military, as Western newspapers have suggested, and more the rise of a kind of military industrial complex. In addition, the introduction of material incentives has exacerbated demands, particularly from lower level bureaucrats and party members, for Western-type consumer goods. The disappointing results of reform and the continued weakness of indigenous innovation have therefore hastened the pressure to acquire Western technology.

A second requirement of the Soviet system is the avoidance of war with the West. Successive Soviet leaders

1. Quoted in Samuel Pisar, *Coexistence and Commerce: Guidelines for Transactions between East and West*, Allen Lane, 1971, p. 27.

have stressed that coexistence with the West gives the Soviet Union a 'respite' in which to raise the level of industrialization, and that avoidance of military conflict with the West is central to Soviet foreign policy. Even Zhdanov, the architect of the Soviet Union's most aggressive post-war international stance, the 'two-camp doctrine', was able to write:

> Soviet foreign policy proceeds from the fact of the coexistence for a long period of the two systems – capitalism and socialism. From this it follows that co-operation between the USSR and countries with other systems is possible, provided the principle of reciprocity is observed and that obligations once assumed are honoured.[1]

In his last publication before his death, *The Economic Problems of the USSR*, Stalin argued that war between the imperialist and Soviet camp was not inevitable.

More important than what Soviet leaders say is what they do. In their attempts to persuade Communist parties to collaborate with nationalist or bourgeois groups, such as in China in the 1920s or in France and Italy in the 1940s, and in their failure to support revolutionary groups within the US sphere of influence, as in Latin America or South East Asia, except Vietnam, it can be assumed that fear of war with the West was the overriding consideration. Similarly, in perhaps the most important confrontation of the post-war period, the Cuban missile crisis, it is significant that it was the Soviet Union which retreated.

These two requirements – Western technology and avoidance of war – have been met through varying methods in the post-war period and this has been reflected in the changing emphasis of Soviet foreign policy. In the late 1940s, the Soviet Union colonized Eastern Europe. The countries of Eastern Europe provided a buffer between the Soviet Union and the West and the advanced industries of East Germany and Czechoslovakia provided a new source for technology. This was the period of greatest

1. Quoted in Marcuse, op. cit., p. 57.

hostility towards the West, of the Two-Camp Doctrine, in which the Soviet Union abandoned the policy of collaboration and confined its political support to Communist parties. Some historians have argued that this stance was imposed on the Soviet Union by the Truman Administration's unwillingness to envisage a neutral Europe and to grant aid for reconstruction on terms that were consistent with defence of the Soviet system.[1]

From 1946 to 1953, Soviet trade turnover with other Comecon[2] countries increased from $800 million to $4,800 million. In addition, the Russians demanded huge reparations – $10,000 million from East Germany, about $2,000 million from Romania, and substantial amounts from Hungary, Czechoslovakia and Poland. Most of this took the form of the physical transfer of industrial and military equipment. From Romania, for example, it is said that the Russians took the entire war fleet, most of the merchant marine, half the available railway stock, all motor cars and a large part of the industry's oil equipment.[3] But ultimately this policy was counter-productive. As the Soviet system was transferred to the Eastern European countries, the technological gap between the Soviet Union and its industrial colonies narrowed and political dissatisfaction grew. This dissatisfaction was expressed in the workers' uprising in Berlin in 1953 and the revolutions in Poland and Hungary in 1956.

The difficulties in the satellites and the weariness of terror produced dramatic changes in policy after Stalin's death. The Soviet leaders, under Malenkov, attempted to revert to the post-war alternative of a neutral Europe. They proposed the reunification and neutrality of Germany and they relaxed controls throughout Eastern Europe; that

1. See Horowitz, *From Yalta to Vietnam*.

2. Comecon is the Council for Mutual Economic Assistance, now comprising Bulgaria, Czechoslovakia, East Germany, Hungary, Poland, Romania, the Soviet Union, Outer Mongolia and Cuba. North Korea and North Vietnam attend meetings as observers. Yugoslavia participates in some activities.

3. For details of reparation payments, see Chris Harman, *Bureaucracy and Revolution in Eastern Europe*, Pluto Press, 1974.

they were serious is indicated by the fact that they warned the East German Communist regime of its impending liquidation. The initiative failed and the liberal conditions gave rise to protest long suppressed. When Khrushchev replaced Malenkov in 1955 he pursued a more modest approach to peaceful coexistence which attempted to combine the use of Eastern Europe as a strategic buffer and a source of resources (not necessarily technology) with a policy of appeasement towards the West. This has broadly represented Soviet policy ever since.

One element of this approach was the new emphasis on trade with the West. Intra-bloc trade declined rapidly from 85 per cent in the years 1951–5, to only 55 per cent in 1961–5. And since then, the importance of Western trade has been increasingly stressed by Soviet leaders. Kosygin told the 23rd Congress that: 'In our time it is becoming more and more evident that the scientific and technical revolution under way in the modern world calls for freer international contacts and creates conditions for broad economic exchanges between socialist and capitalist countries.'[1] And even more striking was Gromyko's appeal, in his opening address to the European security conference at Helsinki, for 'unrestricted, I emphasize, unrestricted, business relations with capitalist countries.'[2]

These statements have elicited an enthusiastic response from Western business. The opening up of the Soviet market occurs at a time when home markets are failing to grow as much as expected and when international competition is intensifying. It is interesting to note that, in the early phase of renewed East–West trade, it was one of the least competitive Western nations, Britain, that took the initiative in selling the socialist countries all manner of goods from copper tubes to complete plants. According to Samuel Pisar, the East–West trade consultant to David Rockefeller, 'the existence near by of a large rapidly developing and presumably non-cyclical market, stretching

1. Quoted in Pisar, op. cit., p. 52.
2. Quoted in Michael Kaser, 'Comecon's Commerce', *Problems of Communism*, July–August 1973.

towards the Urals and beyond, could not but whet the appetites of the surplus-producing Western manufacturers.'[1]

Over the last ten to fifteen years, East–West trade has grown much faster than trade within the East or within the West and important pillars of Western culture, such as Pepsi Cola, have been introduced into the socialist environment. In addition, Western countries have provided substantial credit to the Soviet Union and Eastern Europe.[2] Poland, Romania and Hungary have all joined GATT (the General Agreement on Tariffs and Trade) which places them in a similar trading relationship to the West as Western countries.

Alongside the increase in Western trade, the Soviet Union has also encouraged an increased degree of economic integration among Comecon countries, through the coordination of national plans, the creation of multinational trading associations, and, more recently, through measures to create a 'collective currency' for Comecon countries. Indeed, East–West trade and industrial cooperation has been explicitly linked to economic reform and Comecon integration. This is explained in terms of the need to optimize the use of Western technology through specialization and efficient economies of scale and to raise the technical level of East European exports to the Soviet Union. But it could also be argued that economic integration minimizes the risk that East European countries would develop independent economic ties with the West, a possible precondition for political independence. A typical example was Soviet pressure in 1971 to prevent a Japanese deal with Hungary for the production of Hondas. Instead, the following year, Hungary agreed to produce components for the Soviet Fiat.

A second element in the post-1955 policy was the

1. Pisar, op. cit., p. 47.
2. Japan provided the Soviet Union with $160 million to buy Japanese equipment for the timber industry, to be repaid in timber. Poland received a $300 million credit for eight years, to finance a deal between Massey-Ferguson and Ursus. West Germany made a bond issue of 100 million DM for Hungary in 1975.

support provided to non-aligned governments in the Third World. Some would say that arms and aid represent the most telling evidence for Soviet expansionist ambitions. Yet it can be argued that this was simply a method of fulfilling the Soviet system's second main requirement – the avoidance of war with the West. In particular, with increased East–West exchange, there was an increased risk of Western support for East European dissidents and the prospect that this might provoke war. Through breaking the Western monopoly in the Third World, the Soviet Union aimed to bring about détente, to force the West to agree to the principles, eventually established in 1972 – avoidance of war and mutual non-interference. Soviet newspapers claim that Soviet military strength, for example the overseas deployment of the navy, is a necessary part of détente since it deters Western military intervention in the Third World; though, of course, this justification should be treated as sceptically as the Western bargaining chip excuse for acquiring more arms.

Initially, there may have been an economic motive for the Third World offensive. The Soviet Union could make use of an outlet for heavy machinery and related products that could not compete or were prohibited in Western markets and this became more important after the split with China. Indeed, during the 1960s East–South trade was the most rapidly growing component of world trade; between the mid 1950s and the mid 1960s, the Third World absorbed 25 per cent of the growth in the East's exports. But it was still very small, it did not reach its targets, and towards the end of the decade, dissatisfaction was being expressed by all partners.

The unwillingness – or inability – of the Soviet Union to extend large amounts of credit meant that the socialist countries were forced to absorb often unwanted commodities in payment for their exports. Except in a few cases where raw materials were in short supply or where, as in the case of natural gas from Iran and Afghanistan, imports could be resold to the West for hard currency, the products of underdeveloped countries were competitive with those of the East. Furthermore, the prospects for increasing the market for Soviet goods are diminishing. Without credit or suitable exports, the Third World countries cannot absorb more Soviet plant, equipment or arms. Soviet economists complain of the 'great difficulties caused by the extreme backwardness and limited financial and technical possibilities'.[1]

The Soviet Union still has an important stake in a number of countries – notably Egypt, India and Iraq – and the purpose of such spectacular projects as the Aswan Dam and the Helwan steel complex in Egypt, or the Euphrates Dam in Syria, was as much political as economic – to demonstrate the fact of a viable alternative to dependence on the West. Equally, Soviet support for liberation movements, including the Cuban intervention in Angola, where this does not entail the risk of military confrontation with the United States, can be interpreted in this way.

But again it would be wrong to interpret this political Soviet interest in the Third World as expansionist. There is only one known instance where the Soviet Union has used military and economic aid to exert political pressure.[2] In general, Soviet advisers have been strictly segregated from local politicians and Soviet aid has even been extended to governments which persecute the Communist party. Furthermore, Soviet aid has only proved possible in those areas, like the Middle East or South Asia, where a certain degree of independence is guaranteed by the divisions within the Western world. Arms to Africa or, more recently, Peru, reflect the erosion of exclusive spheres of influence. Soviet penetration of the Third World represents a threat to the West only in the sense that it exacerbates existing tendencies for disintegration. It can be said to be conditioned by and dependent upon Atlantic rivalries.

1. Quoted in Michael Kidron, *Pakistan's Trade with Eastern Bloc Countries*, Praeger, New York, 1972, p. 13.
2. This was Iran in 1963 and may have had as much to do with the Kurds and, hence, geopolitical considerations as with the Communist party. See SIPRI, *The Arms Trade with the Third World*, Almquist & Wicksell, Stockholm, 1971, Chapter 17.

The argument that Soviet policy in the Third World is essentially defensive, aimed at weakening the American monopoly, is also suggested by the Soviet use of Atlantic rivalry. This is evident in the independent political approaches to West European governments – the Treaties of Friendship with France and West Germany – although it may not have been a conscious policy. More recently, the Soviet Union has made use of Atlantic economic competition, although again this may have more to do with terms of deals than with political manoeuvre. American trade with the Soviet Union has never been as large as European trade[1] largely on account of continued American restrictions.[2] The Soviet Foreign Trade Minister, Nikolai S. Patolichev, told a press conference in Washington that a Senate decision to withhold credit from the Soviet Union would be a 'decision to reorient our interests to Western Europe . . . It is for you to judge whether that is in the interests of the American people'.[3] In other words, Soviet leaders seem to recognize that détente and Atlantic rivalry are two complementary elements in the American retreat to parochialism.

Indeed, there is an interesting parallel in the shift of Soviet foreign policy in the mid 1950s and the American shift to parochialism in the early 1970s. The repressive and aggressive Soviet stance in the immediate post-war period was paid for by the East Europeans; the cost of repression returned to the Soviet Union in the form of reparations and unequal trade terms. From the mid 1950s, this became more difficult; technologically, the East European countries had lagged behind and dissatisfaction increased the cost of

1. In 1975, total Western exports to Eastern Europe amounted to $20 billion, of which the US accounted for $2·8 billion ($1·8 billion being payment for wheat and other farm products).

2. These include the unwillingness of Congress to authorize Most Favoured Nation status for the Soviet Union, until the Soviet Union allows free emigration for Jews and the refusal by Co Com (a committee for operating quantitative controls and embargoes on the Soviet Union set up after the war) to authorize two computer deals with the Soviet Union in 1974.

3. *International Herald Tribune*, 28 February 1974.

repression.[1] The alternative was trade with the West and an attempt to exchange repression for détente. This policy, like American parochialism, however, provoked polycentric tendencies within the Soviet bloc (not only in Eastern Europe but in China and South East Asia as well). Despite the use of various devices, such as economic integration, the Warsaw Pact remains the primary instrument for holding Eastern Europe together and, on occasion, the Soviet Union reverts to repression, justified by the charge of Western aggression, as in Czechoslovakia in 1968. Like the dilemma of American policy-makers between parochialism and internationalism, Soviet leaders are pulled by peaceful coexistence, on the one hand, based on the need for Western trade and détente, and by the ritual hostility towards the West, demanded by the suppression of polycentrism on the other. It is probably correct to conclude that the Soviet Union is not fundamentally expansionist towards the West and that, for the time being, the policy of peaceful coexistence is genuine, underscored by the need to acquire Western technology and to avoid a war with the West, and brought to fulfilment by the new American parochialism. But is it possible that this policy might shift and the aggressive element in Soviet foreign policy might increase in importance in response to polycentrism at home and abroad and an American reassertion of international authority?

A major consequence of the flourishing East–West trade is the increase in Eastern indebtedness. In 1975 alone, the combined deficit of the Comecon countries with the West was $10 billion, including $5 billion for the Soviet Union and the total hard currency debt for these countries, at the end of 1975, was estimated at $30 billion, of which the Soviet share amounted to $11 billion. It is argued by some that Western know-how and equipment will enable the socialist countries to expand their exports of raw materials. But various indications, such as the import of

1. There is, of course, a contrast in the economic mechanism. The problem for America was the fact that the Western Europeans got ahead.

agricultural products and natural gas and the physical obstacles to petroleum extraction in Siberia, suggest that this prognosis is doubtful. Others have suggested that the Soviet Union could, if necessary, retreat once more into autarchy. But again this notion is belied by the heavy physical investment made by the Soviet Union in the expansion of foreign trade, e.g. the build-up of the merchant marine, and by the requirements of complex modern technology.[1]

Assuming that the socialist countries are unwilling to dismantle important new investment projects, this debt is likely to grow. Western countries (and a good deal of the credit is officially guaranteed) can continue to expand credit lines and, if necessary, reschedule debts or, as is already being suggested, they can impose tighter criteria for credit worthiness and, ultimately, demand the kind of economic and political conditions that now condemn underdeveloped countries to perpetual dependence. The first approach is more likely should parochialism dominate American foreign policy and Western industrial rivalry grow. But if we suppose that the United States re-establishes authority in the name of Western defence, a re-enactment of the cold war with American dominance in such institutions as the International Monetary Fund or the various 'clubs' which determine private banking policies, then we could envisage conditions attached to future credit as impossible to accept as were the conditions attached to the offer of Marshall Aid. If we also suppose that the renewed American offensive provokes further political struggles in Italy and France and a new isolation of the Communist parties, then it might also be possible to envisage Soviet support for these parties, in anticipation, perhaps, of new industrial colonies, or merely, like the support for non-aligned countries, an improved bargaining position. Such support is likely to be interpreted as unwarranted interference in the Western

1. See Marshall I. Goldman, 'Autarchy or Integration – The USSR and the World Economy' in *Soviet Economy in a New Perspective*. A compendium of papers submitted to the Joint Economic Committee of Congress, Washington DC, 14 October 1976.

sphere of influence, a violation of the Basic Principles of Détente. And in this way the East–West confrontation could re-emerge in a frightening direction. Such a scenario is all the more likely if the disruption of Western trade and liberal tendencies in East Europe undermine stability in the Soviet Union and if the internationalist stance of America leads to the neglect of the domestic economy and the politics of corruption, riot and assassination. These are the circumstances – and they are one possible set among several – in which East–West hostility could lose its ritual character and demand human sacrifice.

3 The Corporation and the State

International politics, the stuff of global conflict, is about the behaviour of states; economics, it seems, has to do with the behaviour of corporations. Many people believe that the connections between the two are not of overriding importance. Changes in the rate of economic growth or the balance of trade may irritate foreign relations but they do not determine them. Whatever the economic difficulties, people would argue, the friendship between Western leaders will overcome conflict. America and the states of Western Europe are democratic nations; they share a common culture and a common set of historical traditions. Conflict, it is argued, is based on the adamant opposition of values, as in the conflict with the Soviet Union, or else on ignorance and lack of understanding. Yet attitudes and beliefs are not immutable; they are the product of social background and they change as society changes. Likewise, abstract monetary measurements of economic performance represent the sum of numerous social phenomena. Behind a trade deficit, for example, may stand an entrepreneur fearful at the cost of introducing new ideas and dismayed by the originality of his foreign competitors or a government official unable to finance an aid programme for an under-developed country which also might have helped promote exports as well as his own career. Added up together, these phenomena may amount to social frustration and social conflict which could well yield changes in values, leaders and even the behaviour of states, changes in which international sympathy is eroded by domestic pressures and in which hostility can develop out of social necessity.

If we are to try to understand the connections between economics and politics, we must start with social changes that affect them both. There are certain similarities in the situation of the entrepreneur and the government official; an analysis of those similarities might have a much wider validity and reduce the need for separate detailed studies of the many different phenomena that underlie a trade deficit. One way to do this is to identify certain universal features of what are normally viewed as the primary economic and political institutions, i.e. corporations and states, and to establish, so to speak, principles which govern their behaviour. These principles amount to a framework which limits the possibilities for future action and which may not be perceived by the entrepreneur or the government official themselves. In other words, if we are to pursue an interpretation of current international trends and future Western conflicts, based on the interaction of different social and political systems, it might be worthwhile to start with fundamentals; to look at the corporation and its relationship to the state.

The Growth of the Corporation

Economic expansion, in the West, is founded on the growth of the corporation. The enterprise of individuals, which was what America stood for, has been transformed into the corporate giants – the General Motors, the Exxons, the Du Ponts – of modern industrial life. These are the successes, the firms which survived; along the way, there were also many failures.

Innovation, investment and the market. The threat of failure is what drives the corporation to expand. It operates in a competitive environment – an environment in which new businesses can always be established, products and production processes can always be imitated or improved upon, and markets can always be captured. The corporation must anticipate the activities of rivals, must keep ahead, in order to be sure of a continued existence. 'Survivors must conform to a model of successful business Darwinism, perpetually encouraging new ventures and extinguishing others, hoping perpetually that some new species will be the gunpowder or the nylon of the technological future.'[1]

IBM, for example, conformed to this model. It succeeded by being the first company to introduce the small transistorized second generation of computers, which were more reliable and less expensive than any previous computer. The new computer, IBM's 1401 machine introduced in 1960, 'turned out' according to one expert 'to be the computer industry's equivalent of the Ford Model T, and definitely established its manufacturer as the Great Power in industry'.[2] Today IBM accounts for two-thirds of the value of computers installed in the Western world and for more than half the yearly shipments. Of the nineteen American firms active in the computer industry in 1959, only four managed to survive until 1973.

The IBM story illustrates another aspect of corporate expansion. Innovation costs money. To innovate, the corporation must invest, whether it be investment in a new labour-saving piece of machinery or in a scientist capable of thinking up new ideas for products or improving efficiency. Other things being equal, the greater the investment, the greater the anticipated innovation. Corporations will always have to try to match the rate of investment of their fastest-growing rivals. Yet to invest,

1. Emma Rothschild, *Paradise Lost: The Decline of the Auto-Industrial Age*, Random House, New York, 1973, p. 197.
2. Nicholas Jequier, 'Computers', in R. Vernon (ed.), *Big Business and the State: Changing Relations in Western Europe*, Macmillan, 1974, pp. 198–9.

the corporation must expect to get a return on its investment through the sale of products; it must realize a sufficient surplus over and above the value of capital advanced. If a new product is developed it must sell better than the old product for which it was substituted, otherwise the cost of its development would not be recovered.[1] In practice, this means that innovation both creates and requires continual market expansion.

IBM's model 1401 yielded sufficient revenue to enable IBM to spend $4,500 million on the third generation of computers, based on integrated circuits. Because of IBM's pre-eminence in the market, few other companies could afford to put such resources into a single project and risk failure to wrest the market from IBM. Indeed, any company with less than 10 per cent of the world market suffered a considerable handicap. This is because marketing costs for computers are very high and because production costs decline with the cumulative number of computers installed. The so-called 'experience curve' does not flatten out until 10 per cent of the world market has been gained. Thus, IBM's success was self-reinforcing. 'What happened in fact is that the commercial superiority established by IBM in the early sixties laid the basis for the technological superiority which was to follow.'[2] And vice versa.

The relationship between investment, innovation and market expansion is not just about scale, it also has to do with time. It is because innovations have to be intro-

1. In the short term, a new product or process might increase the rate of profit so that the extra revenue could be obtained without increasing output. This is because the corporation's monopoly over the new innovation enables it to charge a price above that which would yield a normal profit. Such monopoly profits tend to be whittled away over time by competition. Indeed, except in 'pure' cases of monopoly which are rare, corporations dare not charge monopoly prices for fear of encouraging imitation; although, of course, where the cost of imitation is high, profit differentials can exist up to the limits of profits earned by those corporations who can afford the cost. The fear of potential entrants as a price and profit limiting factor is described by Sylos Labini, *Oligopoly and Technical Progress*, Harvard University Press, Cambridge, Mass., 1969.

2. Jequier, op. cit., p. 199.

duced quickly, because they cannot be spread over time, that they require large markets. Investment or accumulation represents additions to productive capacity. The more often such additions are made, the greater their cost in any one period. Or, to put it another way, innovation is the continual replacement of old machinery and products by new machinery and products. The more rapid the process of accumulation, the newer the machinery or the products, and the greater the competitive advantages in the market place. Take assembly-line manufacture, for example, in automobiles or electronics. The manual tasks to be performed are extremely boring and very simple – human labour could easily be automated and replaced by robots. In theory, robots would be faster and less accident- or strike-prone than humans. But changes in product specifications are so rapid that the tasks, however simple, are changed often. Unless a vast market is available to make the introduction of robots worthwhile, the cost of replacing or reprogramming the robots for each new product is prohibitive. The use of robots, known as 'magic hands', at Japan's Toyota factory in Nagoya is both a reflection of the growing market for Toyotas and an anticipation of future growth.

Another example might be found in the aircraft industry. Improvements in the performance characteristics of aircraft reflect continual increases in the number of man-hours needed to design the aircraft. The first Handley Page military aircraft, produced in 1915, required 300 design weeks, which represented the work of six draughtsmen over a period of fifty weeks. The Halifax bombers, which were produced on the eve of the Second World War, required 8,320 weeks, or seventy-one draughtsmen working for 118 weeks. Today, a typical military aircraft will require about 200,000 design weeks, which is equivalent to 800 draughtsmen working for about five years. Without a substantial increase in the market, these inventions would have to be spread over absurdly long time periods. For if design capacity were kept constant, requiring no new investment, the time taken to design a new aircraft would have increased from fifty weeks in 1915 to twenty-eight years in 1939 to 100 years in 1970. Clearly no aircraft manufacturer could have survived with such long lead times. Equally, the example shows the increase in investment and hence market expansion involved in a speeding-up of innovation. If each aircraft had been designed in fifty weeks, the number of men required would have escalated from six in 1915 to 116 in 1938 to 4,000 in 1970. It would take a very large expansion in the market to justify such rapid innovation.

Survival of the fastest. Evidently then the growth of the corporation is self-reinforcing. And in any economy some corporations will grow faster than others. The fastest-growing corporations will replace their machinery and products most rapidly, retaining and improving their competitive positions and earning higher rates of profit. They will be able to reinvest or borrow on the basis of their high profits and thus keep up their rates of innovation and market expansion. By the same token, slower-growing corporations will find it more and more difficult to maintain their positions; their profits will be insufficient to introduce new machines and products as often as their faster-growing competitors, their market shares will shrink, their ability to finance future innovation will decline further. Indeed, since the need to innovate, and hence invest, is based on the expected innovation of the fastest competitors, rapid growth – more rapid than the total market – becomes the condition for survival. The whole process of economic expansion will be an uneven process in which some corporations expand quickly and other corporations decline or are pushed out.

In theory, of course, the more rapid the growth of the corporation, the greater the increase in overall employment and the more rapid the growth of the market. But there is no *a priori* reason why individual product markets should grow at the same rate as the producers for those markets. The growth of an automobile corporation may well create an increased demand for audio-visual equipment rather than cars. Moreover, even if corporations – or individual investors – are sufficiently flexible to move from one market to another, the mechanism reinforces itself. For rapid growth in a particular market, cars in the 1920s, electronics in the 1960s, merely speeds up the growth of the fastest corporations. IBM's dominance in rapidly expanding computer sales bears testimony to this fact.

Survival of the fastest, moreover, is not simply a question of market expansion; it is also a quest to reduce the cost of production. The permanent effort to make as much profit as the most profitable competitor involves a constant search for cheaper raw materials and machines and a constant pressure to keep wages and overheads low. The elimination of competitors helps to cut costs and increase efficiency through the destruction of excess productive capacity, the devaluation of fixed installations previously acquired, and the more rapid phasing out of older plant and machinery. It may also increase control over suppliers of raw materials and equipment and even the market for labour. All this makes it possible to increase the output per unit of outlay, to increase the overall rate of profit and lay the basis for future investment and growth.

How this operates in practice will, of course, vary from industry to industry, depending on market structure. The so-called 'competitive' industries are distinguished by ease of entry. These include the older industries, like textile, or service industries, like restaurants, chemists or grocery stores, garages, hairdressers, etc. They are generally labour-intensive; it is fairly easy to borrow the necessary capital from the local bank to establish a new launderette or coffee bar. No enterprise can earn more than a minimum rate of profit for very long. A new innovation can always be imitated and cost advantages will be whittled away by lower prices or higher selling costs. And, precisely because competition keeps the profit rate to a minimum, those enterprises which fail to innovate make losses and are forced out of the market. Such industries have a rapid turnover of enterprises; they tend to be characterized by frequent bankruptcies and by large numbers of new entrants. There are the success stories – the Woolworths and the Howard Johnsons – and these are what gradually transform competitive sectors into oligopololy.

The distinguishing feature of oligopolistic competition is difficulty of entry. The initial capital needed to start a new enterprise may be so big that only large corporations or governments can afford to enter the industry (banks are unlikely to risk their loans on individuals lacking established backers). In such industries, rather wide profit differentials can exist and, for longer or shorter periods, fast- and slow-growing corporations can share the market. In the short term, it may not be worth the effort for the fast-growing corporation to reduce prices or increase selling costs, thus lowering its profit margin, in order to eliminate the slow-growing firms. (This may not only be a straightforward profit calculation; it might be necessary to avoid the possible consequence of anti-monopoly legislation.) But such a situation is inherently unstable. Any increase in profit margins, due to a new innovation or an expansion of the market, will introduce the risk of new entrants. And any fall in the profit margin, due to a decline in the overall market or an increase in the cost of labour, raw materials or machines may make it necessary to increase overall profits to maintain the rate of investment. Either possibility will encourage the fast-growing firms to eliminate competitors and capture a larger share of the market. The fastest-growing firms judge their rates of profit, innovation, investment, and growth in terms of their fastest-growing competitors – the rivals which have the resources to enter their markets. For this reason, the process of industrial concentration is catching. Any single firm's decision to eliminate a slow-growing competitor must be copied, lest it gain decisive advantages.

Industrial concentration of this kind infected the Western industrial nations in the late 1960s. In 1965–9, there were over 8,000 mergers in the United States, compared with around 4,000 during the previous five years – itself a high figure by historical standards. In 1968 and 1969 alone there were 4,700 mergers, the assets acquired being worth, in value terms, nearly $25,000 million.

In France, during the same two years, 8,000 companies were involved in mergers; while in Britain, an unprecedented merger activity occurred in 1967 and 1968. In terms of values of companies acquired, the extent of merger activity equalled that of the six years, 1961 to 1966, and was twice that of the seven previous years, 1954 to 1960. In a survey of firms involved in this activity, the majority gave 'fashion', 'defence', and the 'pressure of competition' as explanations. By this they meant that 'once the merger movement was under way, it became necessary for other firms to merge . . . to preclude the possibility of being taken over' or of 'being "weaker" either in a general feeling of relative decrease in market power or in the real threat of a higher level of competition being offered by the merging firms'.[1]

Overseas expansion. Concentration is not the only route through which corporations grow faster than the domestic economy. Another is overseas expansion. This becomes the more important as the possibilities for domestic concentration narrow. The fastest-growing corporations judge their competitiveness internationally. While Japanese corporations have experienced the fastest rate of growth in the capitalist world, the differences between the rates of growth of American firms and the rates of growth of European firms have not been greatly significant. What has varied is the difference between the rate of growth of the fastest corporations and the rate of growth of economies as a whole. Thus the United States and the UK have experienced relatively slow overall rates of growth since the war. The growth rate of the fastest corporations has been achieved partly through industrial concentration, i.e. mergers and takeovers, and partly through expansion overseas. An analysis of the 500 largest US corporations, undertaken at the University of Cambridge, England, showed that a quarter of their growth was achieved through overseas expansion. Of the domestic growth, one third was

1. Gerald Newbould, *Management and Merger Activity*, Guthstead Ltd., 1970, p. 111.

explained by increased concentration. The analysis also showed that the 'giants', the 100 largest corporations, relied much more heavily on overseas expansion. These corporations grew 1 per cent faster than the domestic economy, the extra growth being achieved largely from overseas activities. The corporations in the 100–300 range, on the other hand, grew 4 per cent faster than the national economy, and substantially increased their share of the domestic market. From this it was inferred that the giants 'were unable to increase their share of the domestic economy and compensated partially for their stagnant share by expanding overseas'. Furthermore, the study concluded, if political and economic obstacles hinder domestic concentration in the United States and if 'the economies of the other advanced capitalist countries continue to grow substantially faster than the US economy, big American firms will have to expand overseas at a higher rate if they are not to be overtaken by their rivals'.[1]

But the growth of domestic economies is not independent of overseas expansion. Overseas expansion can take two forms: the export of capital (investment) or the export of goods (exports). Exports make a direct contribution to the domestic economy. They increase production and hence income and employment. Investment contributes to the domestic economy only if profits are repatriated and reinvested at home and if it leads to an increase in exports; otherwise, investment can represent a boost to foreign production and a net drain on the resources available for domestic production. Slow-growing economies, like the United States and Britain, tend to export capital and this further slows their growth; fast-growing economies like Germany and Japan, tend to export goods, speeding up their economic growth.

Indeed, overseas expansion can be treated as a form of geographical concentration, in which some areas

1. Rowthorn, in collaboration with Hymer, 'International Big Business, 1957–67: A Study of Comparative Growth', University of Cambridge, Department of Applied Economics, *Occasional Papers*, 24, Cambridge University Press, 1971, pp. 80, 86.

gain at the expense of others. It is part of the process of industrial concentration, since it involves the elimination of inefficient competitors whose plant is located in unprofitable regions. The criteria for profitability include such things as the size of the local market, nearness to efficient suppliers with up-to-date products and production processes, a developed urban infrastructure with good communications and social opportunities for managers and their families, relative social stability. In practice, these things are to be found in regions which experience rapid economic growth. Thus, like corporate growth, regional economic growth breeds success.

Just as some corporations grow faster than others, so some economies grow faster than others. Fast-growing economies have a higher rate of domestic investment, possess newer plant and machinery or introduce new products more often, so capturing a larger share of the world market, earning higher profits and keeping up their rates of investment. Slow-growing economies experience declining rates of domestic investment, ageing plant and machinery, and declining shares of the world market. This tendency is apparent in the simple fact that not everyone can enjoy a balance of trade surplus. Fast-growing economies expand their exports faster than their imports; slow-growing economies find it difficult to achieve an export growth that will offset their increased consumption of foreign products. Fast-growing economies can spend their export revenue on new innovations which will further expand their foreign markets and reduce the competition from imports. Slow-growing economies must take steps to reduce expenditure on imports – steps which may involve a further slowdown in domestic growth. When fast-growing economies invest abroad, exports and repatriated profits increase. When slow-growing economies invest abroad foreign production replaces exports, the balance of payments deteriorates, income and employment stagnate and even decline. This is the process known as the law of uneven development.

Uneven Development on a World Scale

From the turn of the century until the end of the Second World War, the American economy grew faster than any other. But after 1950, the direction of uneven development was reversed; the Western European nations (excluding Britain) and Japan grew more rapidly than the United States. These countries enjoyed certain specific advantages. Wages were relatively low; the Nazi era in Germany, for instance, had led to a reduction in real wages and an increase in the length of the working day.[1] Much fixed capital, i.e. plant and machinery, had been destroyed or devalued during the war so that, after reconstruction, productive equipment was younger and hence more efficient than in the United States. Also, in the early post-war years, Europe and Japan were heavily protected from world competition (in practice, American) by tariffs, quantitative restrictions, and physical controls over foreign exchange and raw materials.

But none of these advantages were sufficient to explain the ability of these countries to overtake resource-rich fast-growing America. The primary explanation must be sought in the decline of profitable opportunities for investment at home and the decision of American corporations to locate more and more production abroad, particularly in Western Europe.

It has recently become fashionable to talk about long cycles in the history of capitalism.[2] Each cycle is characterized by a different technology; thus the textile and canal age gave way to shipbuilding, coal and railways and now the automobile, aircraft and petroleum industries are being replaced by electronics and chemicals. Each technology is associated with a different set of producers and a

1. Based on an index of 1929 = 100, the real wage in Germany had fallen to 98 by 1939. In the US, the real wage had reached 132 as early as 1933. In 1938, in Germany, men were working a basic fifty-hour week, despite the fact that a 48-hour week had been introduced in the First World War. See Altvater *et al.*, 'On the analysis of imperialism in metropolitan countries: The West German example', *Bulletin of the Conference of Socialist Economists*, Spring 1974.

2. The idea of long cycles is historically associated with the names of Kondratieff and Schumpeter.

different location. Shipbuilding and railways are associated with Britain, the automobile with America, and electronics perhaps, with Japan and South East Asia. It is not necessary to explain these cycles in technological terms or, as Schumpeter did, in terms of clusters of innovatory activity by entrepreneurs. On the contrary, a sociological explanation is more convincing. America's wealth was founded in the automobile age. American social habits are built around the automobile and similar consumer durables; for example, super highways, suburban housing, garages, drive-in supermarkets and movie theatres.[1] The symbols of American military power became the tank and the fighter bomber, just as battleships and heavy artillery were the war weapons of the British era. The biggest American corporations are petroleum and automobile corporations; they dominate the American economy and polity – on them depends the future of millions of workers and thousands of smaller firms.

It has been observed that, at a certain point in the life-cycle of any technology, it becomes more expensive to innovate. Every extra dollar yields a smaller technical improvement.[2] This does not seem to have to do with any inherent characteristic of knowledge but to do with the structure of technology-producing organizations; rigidities seem to develop in the ideas of designers, in the preferences of particular markets, in the structure of production processes. The Japanese are not just good at making the products of the electronic age. They are better than the British at making ships and better than the Americans at making cars. Japanese shipbuilders do not have to contend with small berths, old-fashioned lofts, traditional craft practices, and ageing ship designers. Automobile manufacturers are not faced with a big car mentality.

An article in *Business Week*, entitled 'The Breakdown of US Innovation',[3] argued that US innovation

1. See Emma Rothschild, *Paradise Lost*.
2. See Erich Jantsch, *Technological Forecasting in Perspective*, OECD, Paris, 1967.
3. *Business Week*, 16 February 1976.

increasingly tends to build on existing technology rather than to extend the State of the Art. As examples, it cited Procter and Gamble's latest product, 'Pringle's New-fangled Potato Chips', launched at a cost of $70 million spent over ten years and General Signal Corporation's re-launched 'Electrikbroom', which has been on the market for twenty years. The article argued that 'radical new ideas tend to get bogged down in big company bureaucracy. This is why major innovations – from the diesel loco-motives to xerography and the Polaroid – often come from outside an established industry'. And yet, according to a study undertaken for the US Department of Commerce, new companies with new ideas are not being formed 'in sufficient numbers to provide jobs and technical products for export which will be needed in the decades ahead'.[1]

In effect this means that at a certain stage in the development of an industry or an economy, the relation-ship between investment, innovation and the market breaks down. The characteristics of a particular location – market preferences, experienced suppliers, appropriate infrastructure – that formerly attracted investors now become obstacles to innovation. Investment no longer yields the expected innovation and consequent market expansion. The decline in the growth of the market leads to increased industrial concentration and overseas expansion generally in the form of investment. Both induce further rigidities, as corporations get bigger and as the structure of production processes, markets and suppliers fails to adjust to modern times, and as domestic resources associated with the dominant technologies get scarcer.

As *Business Week* pointed out, the breakdown in innovation was not simply due to rigidities in organization and external infrastructure, it was also due to the 'complex economic environment' in which Federal R. and D. spend-ing has fallen, costs have risen and 'new product failure rates . . . continue to zoom as high as 80% in some in-

1. Quoted, ibid.

dustries'.[1] What has happened is the classic reinforcing mechanism. The decline in innovation caused corporations to invest abroad which speeded up the growth of foreign economies and slowed down the growth of the domestic economy, leading to a further decline in the opportunities for investment and innovation at home.

In the late 1950s, big American corporations found it more profitable to invest abroad than to undertake the costly structural changes required by innovation for the overdeveloped American market; to export the auto-consumer-based infrastructure rather than to replace it. The markets of Europe and Japan were growing rapidly, labour costs were advantageous and various forms of trade discrimination were limiting the potential for increased exports. In Europe, especially, the creation of a tariff-free area, the European Economic Community, made investment attractive. An American executive told Jean-Jacques Servan-Schreiber, the author of *Le Défi américain*: 'The Treaty of Rome is the sweetest deal to come out of Europe. It's what brought us here. We're happy to be here. We're making money. And we're going to make a lot more.'

Once overseas investment gets going, it is catching, rather like industrial concentration. According to an executive in one multinational corporation: 'Our competitors were going overseas and we were afraid that they would get a headstart in a potentially rich market, or would acquire a cheap source of supply for possible reimport into the US, thus threatening our market position.'[2] From 1958, when the Common Market (the EEC) was formed, until 1973, the book value of American investment in Europe – and this greatly underestimates the true value – rose from $6,691 million to $37,218 million.[3] In 1970, a study of 298 American multinationals, accounting for 66 per cent of all sales, showed that the foreign employment

1. ibid.
2. Quoted in Tugendhat, *The Multinationals*, Penguin Books, p. 58.
3. *The Statistical Abstract of the United States 1975*, US Department of Commerce, Washington D C.

of these companies was growing twice as fast as domestic employment and that overseas earnings accounted for 40 per cent of domestic earnings.[1]

But the consequences were not so good for the American economy. Once corporations begin to invest more rapidly abroad than at home, this contributes to the growth of the overall foreign market, stimulates further investment both by the corporation itself and foreign producers, increases the foreign rate of innovation and enhances the competitiveness of foreign produced goods relative to domestically produced goods. The share of the world market held by domestic producers begins to decline, which reduces the profitability of investment opportunities at home, slowing down the growth of the domestic market, further reducing the incentive to invest, the rate of innovation, and the share of the world market.[2] *Business Week* reported in 1963:

> In industry after industry, US companies found that their overseas earnings were soaring, and that their return on investment abroad was frequently much higher than in the US. As earnings abroad began to rise, profit margins from domestic operations began to shrink . . . This is the combination that forced development of the multinational company.[3]

1. *Special Survey of US Multinational Companies 1970*, NTIS, US Department of Commerce, Washington DC, 1972.

2. This is a description of the effects of foreign investment in manufacturing on slow-growing economies. Clearly, the effects of foreign investment in mining and extraction are rather different. In the one case, the corporation substitutes foreign production for exports. In the other case, the corporation substitutes domestic for foreign ownership of production for imports. The latter may cheapen imports of raw materials, increase overseas earnings, and increase exports of capital goods. While foreign investment in manufacturing will also increase overseas earnings and exports of capital goods, this effect is likely to be offset by a declining share of the world market for that product manufactured abroad and by the fact that for a slow-growing economy increased revenue from foreign operations is more likely to be reinvested abroad or spent on imports than invested at home.

3. Quoted in Baran and Sweezy, *Monopoly Capital*, Penguin Books, 1968, p. 195.

From 1957 to 1962, domestic fixed capital formation, i.e. expenditure on plant and machinery, actually fell. Thereafter, it declined in comparison with previous periods as a proportion of national income. Growth was artificially stimulated by a doubling in military spending during the 1960s; even so, it was lower than in any other developed Western nation, with the exception of Britain. Unemployment remained at 5 per cent or 6 per cent and would have been much higher had it not been for military spending.[1] (Among some groups, i.e. black youths, unemployment reached levels of 20 per cent or more.) The real income of industrial workers failed to increase significantly and actually began to fall in the early 1970s. And finally, American goods lost their competitive edge, undermining the power of the dollar, on which foreign expansion was based.

In 1971, when the United States experienced the first trade deficit for as long as anyone could remember, the US Secretary of Commerce explained:

> Historically, US productivity and productivity growth far outpaced other countries mainly because of large scale import of capital and foreign technology, immigration of skilled adult manpower, growth in markets, high wages which induced labour-saving devices, innovative spirit, lack of rigid traditions, and comparatively low war losses. From 1870–1950, the US rate of productivity growth exceeded Europe by 60% and Japan by 70%. Starting in 1950, the situation was reversed, and US productivity growth now lags well behind Europe and Japan.

> From 1950–65 our productivity growth rate trailed Europe by 35% and Japan by 60%. The trend since 1965 shows an even more rapid decline: US rates trailed Europe by 60% and Japan by 84%. These differentials in rates result both from unprecedented

1. In fact there was a rapid rise in the working population during the 1960s, due to the post-war baby bulge. The point was that growth was insufficient to employ the new hands.

levels of productivity growth in Europe and especially in Japan, and from declines in US productivity growth (1965–69), which was only 1·7% compared with 4·5% in Europe and 10·6% in Japan.[1]

The decline in productivity was particularly important in basic industries such as steel, machine tools and automobiles and in high technology sectors, such as chemicals, electrical apparatus, and electronics. The US failure to innovate was evident in the failure to introduce widely the basic oxygen process for making steel, to adopt standardized integrated circuits for radio and TV sets – all black and white TV sets are now imported – or to match Japanese proficiency in the production of miniaturized ball-bearings. The failure to invest and the resulting production rigidities are evident in the ageing US stock of productive equipment. In 1973, the number of young machines (less than ten years old) was lower than at any time since 1940, after ten years of depression.[2]

The relative advantages of foreign production can be seen by looking at the forms of overseas expansion adopted by corporations in different industrialized nations. For America, the ratio of foreign production to export in 1971 was 3·96. For Britain, it was 2·15, but for West Germany and Japan, it was 0·37 and 0·38 respectively.[3] In other words, the relative competitiveness of goods produced in Germany and Japan made it profitable to penetrate the world market through exports rather than production overseas, while the opposite was true for British and American corporations. And these differences reinforced each other. By the late 1960s, American-based producers were beginning to lose their hold on the domestic market. The automobile industries faced severe competition from

1. Quoted in Seymour Melman, *The Permanent War Economy: The Decline of US Capitalism*, Simon and Schuster, New York, 1975, p. 83.

2. See the McGraw-Hill quinquennial survey in *American Machinist*, 29 October 1973.

3. *Multinational Corporations in World Development*, United Nations, New York, 1973.

small German and Japanese cars as well as American cars produced abroad. In electronics, the striking situation was reached in which the United States became a net importer of American-made products. By 1970, 20 per cent of the market for machine tools and 18 per cent of the market for steel had been penetrated by foreign producers. A balance of payments deficit first appeared in 1957, although the balance of trade remained in surplus until 1971.

The State and the Corporation

The economic processes described above are not independent of politics, of the role of nation states. On the contrary, the very use of such terms as the American economy or Germany and Japan implies the existence of separate geographical markets guaranteed by individual states. The corporations, as the economic actors, need a state to set the scenes and keep the technicians and the audience happy. And in its production, the state will reflect all the various contradictory elements of tradition, enthusiasm and prejudice which characterize society.

The modern nation state and the capitalist system developed side by side. Both had their origins in the current of social change that swept away the feudal landowners and brought into political prominence a new middle class of merchants and individual entrepeneurs. These people transformed society from a stable agriculture-based system of production to one whose fundamental aim was business expansion. They needed the state to guarantee the conditions under which they could carry on their business and to remove any obstacles they might encounter. And as they became more powerful, the state needed them for moral and financial support. Even where, as in nineteenth-century England, the middle classes espoused a liberal *laissez-faire* philosophy, the state had to be strong enough to put these ideas into practice; to break up old established monopolies, for example wool, to abolish paternalistic forms of social protection and hence 'free' the market for labour, or to repeal the tariffs which had formerly protected

agriculture and kept domestic food prices and consequently labour costs above world levels. Over time, the
structure of the state – the government and its various
supporting institutions, the armed forces, Parliament, or
the law courts – came to resemble and reinforce the society
out of which it was created. As the small entrepreneur gave
way to the modern corporation, the nineteenth-century
assemblies and their elected executives became the mass
political groupings and the heavy bureaucratic machineries
of the modern industrial state.

The modern nation state is the product of modern
capitalism. In the internal organization of the government
and various associated national institutions, in the ideas of
the people who work for the state and through the struggle
for control over the political system, the state reflects the
continued dominance of corporations in society. Owners
and managers of big corporations have substantial advantages, through their control over resources, in political
debate and social bargaining. This is not simply a matter of
pressure or influence or subjective interest, it is a process of
historical conditioning, in which the assumptions of government become corporate assumptions, in which the ruling
social principles which limit the behaviour of the state are
the principles of the private enterprise system. These
principles need never be exposed to public confrontation
because they are built into the structure of the decision-
making apparatus. All the different interest groups in
society will have links with this or that office or department,
so that the various political or economic issues of policy-
making will get transformed into 'problems of administration'. In the military sector, for example, long association
between particular manufacturers and particular branches of
the armed forces turns corporate competition into bureaucratic rivalry and, thence, into sophisticated debates about
military doctrines. The American debate about whether a
submarine-based nuclear deterrent has made a strategic
bombing force obsolete can also be seen as a form of rivalry
between the air force and the navy or as competition between Rockwell International, the contractor for the can-

celled B-1 bomber, and Lockheed, the manufacturer of Po-
laris and Poseidon missiles. Joining in the argument will be
various politicians, dependent on corporations for election
funds or for employment in their constituencies. Precisely
because corporations are more powerful than other groups
in society, their influence will be felt more in internal
administrative disputes and in debates between the various
arms of the state and within the main political parties.

Yet the development of the modern state did not
come about gently. The state has always tended to be one
step behind or one step ahead of society. At some historical stages, the state was modernizer rudely encouraging
the pace of capitalist expansion; at other times, the state was
a drag on progress, like the absolute monarchy before the
French Revolution or the city states of Italy after the
widening of the capitalist market. Today, many multinational corporate executives say that the nation state is
obsolete. By this they do not mean that the state is obsolete. They mean that a system of states whose functions and
whose power bases are confined to national markets
inhibits the process of capitalist expansion. As they see it,
a state, like the American state, whose power is based on
the decaying industrial structure of American capitalism
and whose functions are to protect those structures from
the impact of uneven development, must transform itself
into a multinational state in the interests of world capitalism.
By the same token, the power base of national states is being
dissipated by the spread of the multinational corporations
and the ability to carry out the traditional functions of
government is consequently undermined.

The main functions of the state are twofold. First,
the state provides the conditions necessary for corporate
expansion, whereby business profits are reinvested in new
plant and machinery and additional labour, thus adding to
the total product of society and increasing the profits of
corporations. In nineteenth-century Britain, this largely
involved the removal of restrictions on the movement of
goods and labour. (The state, for various reasons, played a
much more interventionist role in France and Germany.)

Today the state contributes to almost every stage of the production process. It lays down the conditions for the hiring, firing, remuneration and employment of labour. It helps to provide credit, investment allowances, subsidies of various kinds for the purchase of plant and machinery. It supports the search for and security of sources for raw materials. It influences market conditions, through direct purchases, indirect taxation, tariffs on foreign competitors, or hire purchase terms. It provides basic infrastructure, such as roads or telephones, for both the production and use of goods. And finally, particularly in the defence and basic services sectors, it has become a producer itself.

Take, for example, the aluminium industry. The growth of consumption of aluminium products is currently the highest among major metals, averaging 8 per cent a year since the Second World War. Aluminium producers depend heavily on governments for financial support in the construction of smelters, which involve very large and lumpy investments, and for easy access to plentiful sources of energy. (Together, charges for fixed capital amortization and energy amount to some 70 per cent of the total costs of aluminium production.) They also need government support for securing access to raw materials – bauxite and alumina. Very often agreements about raw materials are part of some general political or commercial agreement with producer governments. Then aluminium sales are largely dependent on government expenditure; big users of aluminium products are the aeronautical and space industries, transport and communications, building construction, and electricity, all of which are dominated by the government. Finally, in some countries, for example Norway, aluminium enterprises are state-owned. Aluminium is not untypical. Indeed there are many industries – steel, aircraft, computers, for example – where the role of the state is even more important.

Increased economic intervention by the state reflects the growing obstacles that corporations must overcome to retain their dynamism. These obstacles are social obstacles, they represent potential social conflict. The second function of the state is the preservation of a stable society, in which a particular class – the owners of corporations – is dominant, and from which the state derives legitimacy. The state must establish a basis on which it can pass and put into effect laws and regulations; its authority must be accepted by all sections of society. Yet the capitalist system, by its very nature, is a society in conflict. Fundamental to the system is the inequality between employer and employee, between the owner of the corporation and those who work for him; the fact that workers do not control the product of their labour and must bargain for a share. It is a system in perpetual change; an expanding system which, as we have seen, creates increasing casualties that have to be mollified, through welfare measures, or repressed.[1] Workers are displaced, small businesses are pushed out, regions decline. At the same time, all sections of society claim a right to share in the expanded product. The state must mediate competing claims on the basis of established social principles and cope with discontent. The post-war period has witnessed an enormous increase in social expenditure – health care, housing, unemployment benefits, education and so on – as well as increased expenditure on the police and armed forces. The size of overall expenditure might be explained in terms of corporate expansion, the need to provide a larger market for corporate growth.[2] But the real nature of public spending must be understood in terms of the need to legitimate the power of the state.

The need to preserve relative social harmony, as it is sometimes described, may contradict the needs of corporate expansion.[3] In certain circumstances, the state may

1. A neo-Fascist state like Franco's Spain will depend primarily on the instruments of coercion to stifle protest, while a Social Democratic state like modern Sweden will tend more towards welfare.

2. It can also be argued that this is offset by the charge on present and future accumulation for financing this expenditure.

3. Recent studies on the role of the state in modern society, undertaken in West Germany, have emphasized the contradictory functions of the state in supporting corporate expansion and preserv-

have to curb some forms of corporate expansion in the interests of social harmony. In particular, a conflict develops from the geographical limitation of the nation state. For the corporation, expansion knows no national bounds. Yet the state derives legitimacy, for the most part from a society located within a particular geographical region, the nation. Taxes are collected, votes are canvassed and soldiers are recruited from within the boundaries of the nation. It is true that powerful states, like the United States of America, can extract resources and promises of various kinds from foreign nations but this depends on the continued strength of a domestic power base. The problem arises when one important section of society, notably the multinational corporation, spills over national boundaries so that state power, confined to the nation, is correspondingly weakened. To put it in another way, if certain sections of society can evade social rules and regulations, then the extent to which the state can curb their actions in the interests of social harmony is reduced. As we have seen, the rise of the multi-national corporation is an important element in the un-evenness of world capitalist development. In slow-growing regions, overseas corporate expansion has resulted in stagnation and unemployment, in protest from workers displaced by foreign investment and imports and from small businesses squeezed by the declining rate of economic growth. Yet at the same time the ability of nation states to curb overseas corporate expansion in the interests of domestic consensus and state power has increasingly been eroded. This contradiction may appear as a fiscal crisis. Because of slow economic growth, the state cannot raise sufficient resources through taxation, borrowing, etc., to finance the growing tasks demanded by society.

Take, for example, the balance of payments. The increase in foreign investment and the declining competitiveness of domestic goods on the world market are likely

ing relative social harmony and have developed analytical concepts to describe them. These concepts, translated into English as 'accumulation' and 'legitimization', have been explored by James O'Connor in *The Fiscal Crisis of the State*, St Martin's Press, New York, 1973.

to involve a balance of payments deficit. That is to say, a nation experiencing relatively slow economic growth is likely to spend more than it sells abroad. The state, as guarantor of the national market and national currency – essential conditions for corporate expansion – must take steps to reduce such a deficit if foreigners are to continue to provide credit and accept the national currency. The state can reduce spending on foreign products or it can alter the relative advantages of domestic versus foreign production so that people, both at home and abroad, buy more domestic products and fewer foreign products. In effect, it can attempt to reverse the direction of uneven development. However, where domestic corporations are also foreign producers, such attempts are likely to be resisted and may well become increasingly ineffective.

The instruments available to nation states for this purpose can be roughly classified under three heads: monetary policy, fiscal policy, and changes in the exchange rate.[1] Both fiscal and monetary policy are designed, primarily, to reduce the overall level of spending – investment, consumption, or public expenditure – in an economy. This will reduce imports and free resources for the production of exports. Monetary policy means expanding or reducing the supply of money (cash or bank deposits) through changes in interest rates or credit restrictions. A rise in the interest rate is expected to attract funds from abroad. It is also supposed to encourage savings and discourage investment and consumption through increasing the cost of borrowing. Economists disagree about the importance of these effects but, in any case, the large, multinational corporation can insulate itself from them. This is because big companies finance their investments from retained earnings or through borrowing from the international banking system – dollar holdings in Europe, for example. They are hardly affected,

1. What follows is a summary of an article by Robin Murray, 'The Multinational Corporation and the British Economy', in J. M. Samuels (ed.), *Readings on Mergers and Takeovers*, Elek Books, 1972. A similar argument can be found in Stuart Holland, *The Socialist Challenge*, Quartet Books, 1975.

therefore, by a change in one nation's interest rate. Furthermore, direct controls on foreign exchange have proved ineffective. An official expert on Euromoney has concluded: 'Lately, the official sector (has) begun to realize that the internationalization of private transactions has progressed to such a degree that some way is always found to circumvent these controls or to force further and increasing corrective action to be taken.'[1]

Fiscal policy has a more direct effect on spending through changes in the rate of taxation. A multinational corporation, however, can avoid direct taxation through the mechanism of transfer pricing: that is, by juggling royalties, licence payments, or the prices of internal trade, so that profits are made in tax havens like Switzerland or Luxembourg. Corporations with holding companies in Switzerland include, to name but a few, Dunlop-Pirelli (the Anglo-Italian tyre company), Michelin (the French tyre company), St Gobain (the French glass-making company), Renault, Olivetti, Montedison, Solvay, BASF and Bayer, the German chemical companies, and the American international companies, Chrysler, Du Pont, Dow Chemical, US Rubber, Singer and Sunbeam. The extent to which transfer pricing can occur is suggested by the fact that in 1970, according to the US Senate Finance Committee, a minimum of 27 per cent of US exports consisted of internal transfers within firms.

In addition to their ability to avoid taxation, the large corporations are less affected by changes in investment grants, initial grants, depreciation allowances and other measures designed to influence the level of investment. This is partly because they have other sources of finance and partly because the size of such grants and allowances as well as tax concessions for foreign corporations, is often fixed at the time the original investment is made.

Changes in exchange rates work in roughly the same way as tariffs and export subsidies – although the use of these as an instrument of national policy was, up to

1. Quoted in Emma Rothschild, 'Banks: The Coming Crisis', *New York Review of Books*, 27 May 1976.

1971, limited by international agreement. A devaluation, or lowering of the exchange rate, means that exports become cheaper in a foreign currency and imports become more expensive in the domestic currency. This should increase the volume of exports and reduce the volume of imports; although it will only apply to manufactured goods since the demand for food and raw materials is relatively static. But the various market-sharing and price-fixing arrangements to which large multinational corporations are subject make them unwilling to expand output from any one particular plant or in any one market. For example, General Motors owns both the British Vauxhall and the German Opel automobile companies; it is unlikely that Vauxhall would make a sustained effort to sell to the German consumer or that Opel would promote its products in Britain. For some companies, notably in the field of computers and agricultural machinery, national production may represent a minor intermediate input in the total production flow – a flow which cannot be altered in the short run. For others, short-term costs may not be the criterion for apportioning production among various foreign subsidiaries. SKF, the Swedish ball-bearing company, has a policy of parcelling out its export orders so as to maintain full capacity in each plant, irrespective of which produces at lowest cost. A company like Philips produces flat irons and mixers in Holland, electric fan heaters in Scotland or cassette tape recorders in Austria; it cannot expand its output of fan heaters, in response to devaluation, if the demand is for cassette tape recorders. Finally, exports may be the subject of an *ab initio* agreement between a foreign firm and the government. This was the case when Chrysler took over Rootes in Britain. In the long term, of course, a devaluation might affect corporate decisions on the location of new capacity; by then, however, the effects of devaluation are likely to be eroded by inflation.

It is not just that multinational corporations fail to respond to devaluation; they can also greatly increase the instability of exchange rates. No multinational company is complete without its department of international financial management and for some companies, notably Esso, Mitsui, and International Harvester, such departments are said to be among the highest profit earners. Not only are most corporations actively involved in speculative activity, but, through speeding up and slowing down trade payments, through borrowing and hedging operations, they had a major impact on the British devaluation of 1967, the French devaluation of 1968, the German revaluation of 1969, and the decision to float the dollar, the pound, the franc, and the lira. During 1967 United Shoe company, a long-standing foreign investor, not only hedged extensively in the forward exchange market against devaluation but also had its various subsidiaries defer payments to the British affiliates for as long as six or seven months. Massey-Ferguson did the same thing. During the franc crisis of 1968, international corporations moved out of the franc to an amount equal to $1,000 million. One US company reduced its holding of francs from $10 million to $100,000 over a ten-month period while another sold 100 million francs forward, a figure which was equal to its total assets in France. An oil company treasurer is reputed to have said that 'when I write a cheque, it's the bank that bounces.'

For these reasons, governments faced with balance of payments deficits are left with those measures which fall most heavily on national producers and labour; namely reductions in public spending and increases in income and purchase tax. (As we shall see below, the United States, because of its international power, does have an alternative.) Such measures will also depress the sales of the big multi-national corporations, but because of their market-sharing arrangements, they can compensate for a fall in output with an increase in price. Indeed – and this is another factor accounting for the failure of big corporations to respond to government measures designed to affect the level of investment – in the highly advanced sectors, such as chemicals or electronics, the gestation period for new products or new methods of production is so long that investment plans are made several years in advance. A large corporation cannot afford to jeopardize such plans for the sake of short-term national stabilization measures. Because these plans are financed out of retained earnings, the big corporations find it necessary to raise prices in periods of deflationary policy in order to ensure a steady cash flow.[1]

This phenomenon of 'recession with inflation' was first observed in the 1957–8 recession by Sylos Labini, who argued that while such prices are 'inconceivable under competition, they are not only conceivable but necessary under oligopoly'.[2] This argument is borne out by corporate officials. The President of the Chemical Industries Association explained at its 1970 annual dinner: 'Price increases over a wide range of chemical products are seen as inevitable if the UK industry is to generate the cash flow needed to cope with a rate of expansion that is modest in comparison with all other industrialized countries.'[3] Such price rises further reduce the real spending power of the working population, increase the pressure of money wages, and depress the sales of the small domestic corporation. Since small domestic corporations are most often to be found in the relatively competitive, less advanced, labour-intensive sector, they are more susceptible to the pressure of wages; a deflationary policy will reduce their competitiveness and force many of them out of business.

In resorting to deflation to correct the balance of payments, governments utterly fail to reverse the direction of uneven development. On the contrary, market expansion is slowed, investment opportunities decline, innovation gets further behind and, in the long run, the balance of trade continues to deteriorate. Because of the multinational erosion of state power, the state, despite itself, becomes a participant in the process of overseas expansion and uneven development, exacerbating the tendencies for stagnation,

1. This argument was propounded and explored by Charles Levinson in *Capital, Inflation and the Multinationals*, Allen & Unwin, 1971.

2. Labini, *Oligopoly and Technical Progress*, p. 81. He explains that 'oligopolistic producers do not have to take price as a datum fixed impersonally by the market, but can influence price by quickly reducing output in response to a contraction in demand'.

3. Quoted by Levinson, op. cit., p. 177.

inflation and unemployment, undermining social harmony. Every attempt to curb overseas corporate expansion in the interest of national consensus recoils in increased conflict. The problem is the narrow basis of state power compared with the widening spread of corporate activity. The solution would seem to be the multinational state but like the city states and the nation state, it is not likely to come about without unpredictable political convulsion.

For smaller nation states, it means dissolution. It means the creation of new super states like Europe or Atlantica, where peripheral protest and conflict will be submerged in a wide multinational society.

For America, it could mean a sort of self-transformation. The United States can substitute a kind of imperialism for deflation; it can extract resources from foreign countries and extend the territorial range of state power. The American state could become a new multinational state. In a sense, this has already occurred. Since the war, as we shall try to show in subsequent chapters, the American state has acted as guarantor for world corporate expansion, providing an international currency – the dollar – dismantling trade barriers, stimulating world output through aid, etc. It has also attempted to uphold its international legitimacy – preserving relative harmony with soldiers and economic advisers. But this role has always contained a fundamental contradiction, in that the American state has not become a truly multinational state. Its power is still the power of American capitalism and it exercises power in the interests of American capitalism. So long as the American economy grew faster than any other, the interests of American and world capitalism were the same. Now this is no longer true and the parochial nature of the American state has become apparent.

In the last few years, the international authority of the United States has become a brake on world corporate expansion and a provocation to social conflict all over the world. In effect the United States has used its international authority to export domestic American problems. As we shall see, the various crises of recent years were not chance events. They were the consequence of American attempts to solve the balance of payments problem without or with the minimum of domestic deflation; they were the consequence of the diverging directions of the American economy and the world economy. The decision to reduce economic and military aid, for example, was a major factor in the enormous increase in the sale of food and arms. These crises did not reverse the direction of uneven development, but they slowed down world economic growth. The rise in the cost of food and energy and the increased expenditure on armaments reduced the overall demand for manufactured goods and, hence, the rate of investment in manufacturing activities and increased investment in less productive activities such as armaments or inefficient sources for food and energy. The crises also set in motion a series of political crises. The burdens of the American economy are being borne by foreign workers and small foreign producers. Indeed, the more American policies slow down world economic growth, the greater is likely to be the foreign protest, the fragmentation of power, the dissatisfaction of the multinational corporation operating in an unstable world, and the emergence of competing multinational states such as Europe.

In the end, the crises will affect America itself. For the increased cost of international authority, the cost of renewed aid and repression, the cost of preventing cheap, alternative sources for food or arms, offsets the improvement in the American economy. The prognosis is gloomy: increased repression at home and abroad, social conflict and economic crisis as the American state attempts to save itself, sometimes in the guise of a multinational state and sometimes frankly parochial.

4   Money

How will these abstract developments unfold in practice?
How has American behaviour caused the crises of the
last few years? What do the changing relations between
corporation and state imply for real observable politics?

    These questions could be looked at through various
media. A starting-point is money. Money as an issue
embraces all other issues. The international movement of
money could be treated as the sum total of the movement
of other things – trade, investment, aid and foreign military
expenditures. Just as the sovereignty of the nation state –
its ability to guarantee the conditions for corporate expansion and its continued legitimacy – is perhaps personified
in its ability to create money, so the world order is personified by the form and status of international money. International monetary crises are no more than the expression of
changing power relationships. Today's monetary muddle
reflects uncertainty about the future of international politics; no one knows whether there will be a world of competing monetary blocs or a reassertion of the old dollar-
based system.

At Bretton Woods in 1944, forty-four nations met to plan the post-war money system. What they established – which was quite different from what they conceived[1] – was a system which gave the United States the power to create money and established the Federal Reserve as the world's central bank. For a quarter of a century, the dollar fulfilled the essential prerequisites of international money; it was acceptable as a means of payment and its supply, through aid, military expenditure, and private investment, expanded along with economic activity. So long as people wanted to buy American goods with the dollars they accumulated, the system worked well.[2] But as people began to spend their dollars, not on American goods, but on German and Japanese goods, the acceptability of the dollar as a means of payment was increasingly called into question. The growing US deficit and the suspicion, based on the growing challenge to American power, that the writ of the dollar could no longer be enforced, marked the downfall of the Bretton Woods system.

Under the practice of this system, national currencies were tied to the dollar, which in turn was tied to gold. Certain currencies, notably those belonging to members of the British Commonwealth, were tied to sterling – a remnant of an era when the Bank of England was the bank of the world. International payments and international reserves (assets kept by central banks to back national currencies and to make payments in case of foreign deficits) were made up of gold, sterling, and dollars – and increasingly the latter. For most of the period, the exchange

1. The Bretton Woods system was supposed to be truly internationalist. There were to be rapid balance of payments adjustments through exchange rate changes and temporary assistance to countries in deficit was to be provided by an international central bank, the International Monetary Fund (IMF).

2. This is how the gold standard functioned before 1914. An outflow of British capital in the form of investment and military spending helped to increase British exports and, hence, finance further outflows. The size of the current surplus and the size of capital outflows tended to move in the same direction.

rates, or 'parities', as they are called in international monetary parlance, of the currencies of Western industrial nations, in terms of the dollar, remained fixed and, from the late 1950s, these currencies were fully convertible, i.e. they could be freely exchanged for an equivalent amount of dollars or gold.

In addition, the conference at Bretton Woods established the International Monetary Fund, originally intended as the pivot of the system. The Fund provided a modest alternative form of international money under a system of quotas, equivalent to initial subscriptions made by members in gold and in the members' currencies. In 1970, the Fund provided additional international money known as Special Drawing Rights (SDRs), a form of credit backed by quota. Since the United States had the largest quota and since the conditions attached to the use of quotas were rather restrictive, in practice the Fund provided less an alternative and more a reinforcement to the supremacy of the dollar.

Paper dollars are nothing more than IOUs for gold or American goods. It costs nothing to add an extra nought to a 100-dollar bill. But to produce 1,000 dollars' worth of gold or goods involves ten times more effort, or thereabouts, than to produce 100 dollars' worth of good or gold. For dollars to be acceptable as international money, people must believe that the Federal Reserve will not print extra noughts on 100-dollar bills, on a generous whim. They must believe that dollar IOUs will be honoured, that their pieces of paper will be exchangeable for an equivalent amount of goods or gold. This belief rests on either a realistic assessment of the value of the dollar or an American power, a belief that the US government can guarantee a price for the dollar, even if this price does not reflect what people believe to be its true value in goods or gold.

From 1958, the United States began to experience increasingly large payments deficits. This was the period when large American corporations began to extend their manufacturing operations abroad, when domestic growth declined along with the competitiveness of American goods and when Americans began to experience the impact of uneven development. In fact the US continued to enjoy a trade surplus until 1971. But it was insufficient to cover the outflow of capital. This outflow took two forms. The first was private foreign investment which did, of course, yield a return; indeed repatriated profits were twice as large as the annual outflow.[1] The second was American government expenditure, the cost to America, in terms of aid and forces stationed abroad, of maintaining its global position; America was not earning enough to pay for her role as world policeman.

The point was that the dollars acquired by foreigners through US government spending did not return to the US in the form of purchases of US goods.[2] The outflow of dollars should have resulted in an improvement in the US trade surplus. The fact that it did not do so indicated the declining competitiveness of American goods, that the dollars were being spent on goods produced in Europe and other places, whether by US or European corporations. It indicated that one dollar could buy more foreign goods than American goods, i.e. that the dollar was over-valued.

But so long as foreigners were prepared to accept dollars instead of gold or some other currency, so long as they believed that the US would guarantee the value of the dollar in goods or gold or foreign currencies, the over-valuation of the dollar did not matter, the dollar could continue to function as international money and the US balance of payments deficit merely resulted in an expansion in its supply, servicing the expansion of the world economy. But this depended on the international authority of the US government, on the power to insist that parities remained

1. This does not necessarily mean, as some have claimed, that investment makes a positive contribution to the balance of payments. Such a view ignores what is done with repatriated profits – (they may be spent on imports) and what would have happened to the trade balance in the absence of foreign investment (exports might have been larger).

2. Under the gold standard in the nineteenth century, British overseas spending tended to boost British exports.

unchanged, that foreign central banks cooperate in maintaining the value of the dollar. For example, agreements, signed in 1968, concerning the presence of US troops in Germany included a West German pledge that its dollar reserves would not be converted into gold. The elaborate network of foreign relations, shored up by the ability to spend overseas, placed the United States in a position to back the dollar with more than promises.

Here lay the central paradox of the post-war monetary system. American hegemony derived from America's twin roles as central banker and policeman. These roles depended on each other. Only as central banker could the US afford to police the world. Only as policeman could the US guarantee that its dollar IOUs would be repaid, once it became clear that the price of the dollar no longer reflected the value of US goods in terms of gold or foreign goods, and that the Federal Reserve was, in fact, printing extra noughts on 100-dollar bills.

The US role as central banker was threatened from the early 1960s by the growth of the multinational corporation and by the emergence of alternative central bankers in Europe and Japan. The multinational erosion of the American power to create international money took the form of massive speculative activity. In place of the individual, perhaps amateur, small speculator of an earlier era came, as we have noted, the large multinational corporation, which could not afford to be caught short (i.e. with a devalued currency) in case of a change in exchange rates. The destabilizing impact of large well-informed institutions with holdings in several different currencies was very great. As *Business Week* pointed out in explaining the 1973 decline of the dollar:

> Multinational corporations shifted huge balances to their foreign subsidiaries. Banks moved more money to overseas branches. US importers with bills to pay in foreign currencies rushed to settle them before the dollar sank anymore. And overseas buyers of US goods dragged their feet on payment hoping to get the dollars

they needed at a still lower rate ... From the standpoint of the people involved, it looked like plain commonsense.[1]

A new opportunity for speculation arose in the Eurodollar market. This market developed largely from the restrictions placed on capital exports by the Kennedy and Johnson Administrations.[2] Rather than repatriate dollars earned abroad, corporations accumulated dollar balances in foreign banks for reinvestment purposes. The banks then treated these holdings as assets against which to make dollar loans amounting to as much as 90 per cent of the original holding. This process could continue indefinitely, resulting in total Eurodollar holdings many times larger than the original one. For example, a corporation might deposit a cheque for $1,000, drawn on a deposit account at Chase Manhattan in New York, in a London bank, rather than cashing it. The London bank would treat the credit at Chase Manhattan as an asset and would feel free to make a loan of $900 to some other bank or corporation keeping only 10 per cent as a prudential reserve to back the loan. (For foreign currency holdings, there is no legal reserve requirement.) The borrower would, apparently, receive a dollar credit of $900 at a Chase Manhattan account, and would then feel free to make a further loan of $810, and so on. No one knows the precise extent of the Eurocurrency holdings but it is estimated that anything between $150 billion and $250 billion of loose, liquid credit of this type could be floating around Europe, roughly one and a half to two times the size of world reserves. According to the US Senate Finance Committee, a movement of between 1 per cent and 3 per cent of these funds is 'quite sufficient to produce a first-class international financial crisis'.[3]

1. 'Why the dollar falls', *Business Week*, 23 July 1973.

2. These restrictions were imposed partly to improve the balance of payments but more importantly to meet the demands of labour unions who argued that foreign investment represented the export of jobs.

3. *Implications of Multinational Firms for World Trade and Investment and for US Trade and Labour*, Hearings, Committee on Finance, US Senate, February 1973.

The fact that Eurodollar holdings are becoming large enough to topple exchange rates is self-reinforcing, for it convinces holders of dollars that the value of their holdings is no longer secure. The first exchange rate to go was the pound sterling which was devalued in November 1967. The pound had been, in a sense, the front-line of the dollar defence – a sort of absorber of speculative shocks. Once it was devalued, attention was concentrated on the dollar. In March 1968, the United States established a two-tier market for gold, according to which the free market price was allowed to rise while the price at which central banks exchanged gold remained $35. In effect, this amounted to making the dollar inconvertible.

Equally, speculators began to suspect that European and Japanese currencies might be revalued. The decision of the European Community in 1970 to create a single European currency suggested that, together, the Europeans might challenge the dollar, where they had not been able to individually. Together, the nine countries of Western Europe comprised the world's largest trading bloc and their monetary reserves were considerably larger than those of the United States. Starting with de Gaulle, many Europeans were objecting to the over-valuation of the dollar on the grounds that it enabled US corporations to buy up foreign factories and the US government to fight wars and bribe foreign governments on the cheap. More importantly, there was a growing concern about inflation, which was blamed on the over-creation of international money by the United States. Pompidou, as French President, said: 'We cannot keep forever as our basic monetary yardstick a national currency that constantly loses value ... The rest of the world cannot be expected to regulate its life by a clock which is always slow.'[1]

Germany did revalue in 1969 but this was insufficient to slow the rapid rise in prices. Both the German and Japanese governments were, as a consequence of runaway inflations and post-war currency crises, extremely

1. Quoted in Lafeber, *America, Russia and the Cold War, 1945–71*, p. 289.

sensitive to the domestic consequences of inflation. Only the dollar appeared to stand in the way of a solution. And only the US government, in its guise as world policeman, was defending the dollar.

But the US role as world policeman was also being threatened, notably by Vietnam. No one was prepared to pay for the war, and in any case, there was unemployment at home, and so the US government printed money instead. In earlier times, this might have had beneficial effects, but, in the economic conditions of the 1960s, this excessive expenditure on the unproductive activity of fighting abroad failed to stimulate domestic investment sufficiently to meet the increased domestic demand and to enhance the competitiveness of American exports. The result was inflation and the rapid deterioration in the balance of payments. What is more the US had demonstrably failed to police South East Asia and the attempt to rectify this failure was bound to affect the dollar.

Withdrawal from S.E. Asia 'with honour' meant making friends with the Soviet Union and China. A mutual guarantee of non-interference seemed like a cheaper way of being policeman. But détente had a corrosive effect on the Atlantic Alliance. It removed the justification for holding Europe and America tightly together. It removed the *raison d'être* for US troops in Europe and hence the lever to be used in negotiations with European central banks. It is no accident that 1971 was the year Nixon announced his trips to Peking and Moscow, the year of the first US trade deficit in the twentieth century and, also, the year in which the Europeans, with the help of Japan, brought down the dollar.

In May 1971, the Dutch guilder and the German mark were floated.[1] In August, President Nixon announced his New Economic Policy: a prices and wages freeze, a 10 per cent import surcharge, and the *de jure* inconvertibility of the dollar. In December, the Finance Ministers of the

1. The Swiss franc and the Austrian schilling were also revalued.

Western world concluded what President Nixon described as 'the most significant monetary agreement in the history of the world'. At the Smithsonian Institute in Washington, they agreed on an 8 per cent devaluation of the dollar against gold and a realignment of currencies, including a revaluation of the mark by 5 per cent and the yen by 8 per cent. The US deficit continued to deteriorate in 1972, Euro-dollars continued to grow, and the 'most significant monetary agreement' lasted less than fourteen months. In February 1973 the dollar was devalued by a further 10 per cent and, after three weeks of panic, the European exchange markets were closed. When they reopened in mid March, the European currencies, excluding the pound and the lira, were floating as a bloc upwards against the dollar. (And, in January 1974, the franc joined the pound and the lira in an independent float.)

Ever since the Smithsonian Agreement, Finance Ministers have been meeting to develop the outlines of new international monetary systems. At every meeting of the IMF's Committee of Twenty Finance Ministers, decisions are taken to postpone decisions until the next meeting. There is general agreement – with occasional American dissension – that it should be a system of fixed rates with full convertibility into a single international asset based on SDRs.[1] But dollar convertibility can be achieved only if adequate provision is made for balance of payments adjustments and if the problem of Eurodollars can be solved. The first issue is less intractable than the second. The US insists that deflation, i.e. spending cuts as a method of adjustment is out of the question; instead provision must be made for rapid exchange rate changes in case of balance of payments disequilibria and automatic sanctions against countries persistently in surplus. Neither of these options is entirely satisfactory to those European countries which

[1]. The French would like a system based on gold. But like the original gold standard, such a system could only operate effectively in conjunction with other currencies. It would either be a new dollar-based system or a system of competing currency blocs.

have enjoyed long-standing surpluses. Moreover, so long as the Eurodollars remain in existence, the possibility of exchange rate changes is likely to encourage speculative flows and bring such changes about. The problem of Euro-dollars can be solved only by their elimination or by the allocation of a sufficiently large amount of SDRs to enable the US to convert excess dollar holdings should it become necessary. The former is unacceptable to central bankers and multinational corporations who, after all, have a large say in these matters. The latter would merely result in a resurrection of the dollar standard under an SDR guise. SDRs could be used to finance US deficits until such time as Euro-SDRs build up to such an extent that the dollar and the SDR is brought down all over again. Only if the US were prepared to accept the discipline imposed on the dollar by a truly international authority could the SDR system function effectively. But that would mean the crea-tion of a truly multinational authority, operating on behalf of world capitalism, preventing self-imposed barriers for the protection of slow-growing regions. Only if the US succeeded in re-establishing its former economic dominance, and, in the process, solving its balance of payments prob-lem, would a new dollar-based SDR standard become a real possibility.

In the meantime, however, the present system of floating monetary blocs is likely to continue. Many Ameri-cans, schooled in the equilibrating mechanisms of free markets, look at this prospect with equanimity. The dollar will float downwards until it finds an equilibrium price at which exports will balance imports, and when the happy day arrives when exports exceed imports, the dollar will float upwards again. Speculators will, in this Utopian world, add to the general harmony by bidding the dollar down if it is above its equilibrium price and up if it is below. This view is not shared in Europe. Giscard d'Estaing argues that the present non-system 'reveals a profound disorganization of the monetary community and marks a step back into anarchy and irresponsibility. No Government which is conscious of the importance of the stability of international

economic relations can consider this situation with light-
ness of heart.'[1]

The crux of the matter is the myth of equilibrium
and the consequent myth, stabilizing speculation. In the
short term, it is true that the American balance of payments
did improve. But it is not at all clear that this was due to the
floating of the dollar. Rather, it can be explained by the
rapid rise in world food prices and the reduction in food
aid which led to a doubling of American agricultural
exports during 1973, to the oil crisis which affected the
American balance of payments less than other countries,
and the enormous increase in arms sales. Unless it is assumed
that food scarcities and arms races are going to be permanent and that alternative cheap sources of food and arms are
not developed, temporary improvements in the trade
balance do not indicate the likely course of events. Indeed,
if the US is to maintain its monopoly position as supplier
of food and arms, some reversion to aid and military intervention must occur, undermining once more the balance of
payments.

Depreciation is not likely to reverse the direction
of uneven development. First of all, the effect of depreciation is less than supposed. It stimulates inflation – although
this has not entirely offset the competitive advantages of
depreciation because inflation has been more rapid in
Japan, France, Italy and Britain. In large areas of manufacturing, prices are fixed by international agreement,
making it impossible for exporters to lower the prices of
their goods on world markets – although, of course, the
extra dollar revenue received might be used to compete
more effectively through quality, advertising, etc. And,
finally, a quarter of US exports consist of capital goods for
US factories overseas. Unless overseas production is
expanded, the fall in prices will have no effect on the volume
of such exports; indeed, in so far as depreciation does
discriminate against foreign production, it could actually
involve a reduction in these goods. The ineffectiveness of
depreciation on trade in manufactured goods is demon-

1. Quoted in *The Times*, 27 July 1973.

strated in the continued growth of Germany and Japan. Despite the revaluation of the Deutschmark, West Germany now exports more manufactured goods than the United States, has twice as many monetary reserves and a higher *per capita* income. In central Europe, a new Deutschmark zone is developing.

On the capital side, the depreciation has enormously raised the cost of overseas investment, aid and military spending. Government expenditure abroad was reduced in any case, as the US withdrew from South East Asia and cut back on aid commitments, although, as was mentioned, renewed internationalism entails renewed expenditure. Foreign investment in the US has increased and American multinationals are faced with the ignominy of mark and yen holders buying up American and foreign factories at bargain prices. In so far as this development could increase the American growth rate, it would require a prolonged and permanent depreciation. This is because the structural problems in the American economy that led American multinationals to invest abroad in the first place have not changed. The dominance of a few big companies, the over-development of consumer markets, the old ideas and equipment for production, still mean that it costs more to innovate in the US and that it is likely to continue to cost more.

Even if the additional cost is offset by prolonged depreciation and even if it is supposed that similar rigidities develop abroad, expansion will ultimately come up against limits imposed by foreigners. The boost to American competitiveness will be achieved through a shift of production from Europe and Japan to America. This means either an increased share of world markets for American-based corporations or an expansion of foreign production as opposed to imports in America. Put in monetary terms, the US surplus will be a European deficit. This was the situation after the Second World War when weak European governments accepted American loans to finance their imports and also accepted American influence in various aspects of policy. And it could become the situation again, if the European Community breaks down. But, if one envisages the creation of an alternative power bloc, a European Union, for example, then the 'export of jobs' reflected in the deficit would be resisted; joint European action might be taken to restrict capital movements, depreciate the Euromark, if it is so called, and control foreign trade. Any one of these measures could spark retaliation. As one American expert has put it: 'Any prolonged and sizeable deviation from a pattern of exchange rates which effectively mirrors current international competitive positions is thus almost certain to trigger economic, and even political conflict.'[1]

This kind of development becomes more likely as crises develop. And crises seem to be the consequence of American attempts to pursue parochial interests.

Gloomy predictions have been made about the destabilizing consequences of the oil crisis. Although industrialized countries recently agreed to avoid unilateral measures to cope with oil-induced balance of payments deficits, it may be difficult to keep to that agreement.

The Achilles heel of the entire world economy may turn out to be the international payments system. The financial flows associated with more expensive oil are so immense as to threaten intolerable balance of payments strains and currency instability. While technical solutions to many, if not all, of the financial problems can be devised, it remains to be seen whether international cooperation will be up to the task of implementing them. The price of failure could be high. To fail would be to risk competitive devaluations and trade restrictions that would amplify recessionary tendencies already set in motion by the energy crisis.[2]

An imminent crisis which could have serious repercussions could occur in the Eurocurrency market. The

1. C. Fred Bergsten, 'New Urgency For International Monetary Reform', *Foreign Policy*, no. 19, Summer 1975.

2. George A. Pollack, 'The Economic Consequences of the Energy Crisis', *Foreign Affairs*, April 1974.

collapse of Franklin National Bank, in the spring of 1974, highlighted the involvement of many banks in commodity speculation. Much of this speculation has been financed by Eurodollar loans. Also, European-based banks have been heavily involved in providing dollar finance to under-developed countries. The indebtedness of underdeveloped countries in consequence of the rise in the cost of food and arms and the decline in aid has reached some $100 billion. Such is the weakness of the Eurodollar base, that it would theoretically only take a minor downward movement in commodity speculation or one default by an underdeveloped country to bring about the collapse of the whole pyramiding Eurodollar system. Such a collapse would affect American banks least, for they can turn to the Federal Reserve for support, which in itself indicates the lack of governmental control over the creation of international money. But European banks may well be forced into bankruptcy. And because of the dependence of corporations on liquid bank credit for working capital (cash for paying wages, etc.), particularly since the rise in input prices and recession in sales caused by the oil crisis, this would threaten the viability of many European and US European-based corporations, not to mention the public borrowers in Britain, Italy and France. The extent to which such a crisis can be avoided will depend on the possibilities for concerted international action, on the ability and/or willingness of the US Federal Reserve to act as a lender of last resort. And this again depends on the future of American power.

The present monetary muddle is inherently un-stable. There is no real international money. The dollar continues to function as a means of payment but it is no longer convertible into gold and its value in terms of American or foreign goods no longer has a credible guaran-tee. Its acceptability as a means of payment – and that of other currencies which can only be converted into dollars or each other – is increasingly called into question. Future crises, caused by panic speculation, can be averted or re-solved only by a new monetary standard, based on gold, some other commodity, or renewed confidence in the dollar.

Any of these will require American hegemony; only America may be powerful enough to impose a new monetary standard on the world. If, however, she is not, if American power is successfully challenged by a European Union, say, then the world of floating money is most likely to turn into economic warfare.

5   Trade

The issue of internationalism versus parochialism has traditionally been conceived in terms of the movement of goods, in terms of free trade versus protection, or liberalism versus mercantilism. In today's world, the movement of capital, the internationalization of production processes, is probably more important in transmitting prosperity or depression from one economy to another, in integrating the world market. Nevertheless, trade has grown enormously since the war and nowhere has it grown faster than within the industrialized regions of the West. An increase in exports relative to imports still represents a gain in income and employment and an increase in imports relative to exports can still be viewed as the export of jobs. The power to dismantle or erect barriers to the free flow of goods still influences the direction of the world economy and, in so far as it represents one of the attributes of national sovereignty, still signals changes in the political constellation.

In particular, the changing balance of power within the West first became evident in trade talks. Conflict with America was of course contained in the very idea of a new subcontinental nation, as rich and as powerful as the United States. Yet Americans have always praised the conception and confined their criticism to the form. Because the form is a customs unions and an agricultural policy, the Euro-American conflict has made its appearance in trade negotiations. Thus trade disputes, which may appear superficial and even niggling, have a significance far wider than the direct economic consequences of lowering one or another tariff. In its negotiating stance, the United States has consistently challenged the essence of the existing European framework.

The New Dealer's post-war vision, articulated by Roosevelt's Secretary of State, Cordell Hull, was a world of free trade and free movements of capital and labour – a world, although this was never made explicit, where American goods and American know-how would capture every market. This vision was destroyed, at an early date, by the poverty of Europe – and Japan – and by the discovery that the bilateral barter agreements and the plethora of controls over money and goods, created during the war and the depression, could not be dismantled without closing the European market for ever. The shock of free trade would have played directly into the hands of the opponents of the capitalist system.

Instead, the United States encouraged the beleaguered European governments to cling together in the European commitment and in the Atlantic Alliance and allowed them to postpone the restoration of currency convertibility and the end of trade discrimination. By the time they were strong enough to fulfil their promises, they were also ready to challenge the industrial supremacy of the United States. The embryo of the challenge was the economic community.

That it was recognized as such is evidenced by Kennedy's call for an Atlantic Partnership and his introduction of the Trade Expansion Act in 1962. In presenting the Act, he told Congress that it

will either mark the beginning of a new chapter in the

alliance of free nations . . . or a threat to the growth of Western unity. The two great Atlantic markets will either grow together or they will grow apart. The meaning and range of free economic choice will either be widened for the benefit of free men everywhere – or confined and constricted by new barriers and delays . . . This bill, by enabling us to strike a bargain with the Common Market, will 'strike a blow' for freedom.[1]

The bargain that Kennedy proposed to make would have dissipated all that distinguished the Common Market. The Act contained the so-called dominant supplier provision which gave the President the authority to eliminate tariffs on products in which the United States and its trading partner accounted for more than 80 per cent of world trade. Had Britain joined the Common Market in 1963, this would have enabled President Kennedy, despite his emphatic denials,[2] to create what amounted to an Atlantic free trade area, without legally violating the Most Favoured Nation clause in GATT, which disallows preferential trade treatment.

In the event, such plans were undermined by the Gallic veto on Britain's entry and the only items which qualified for the dominant supplier provision were aircraft and magarine. Nevertheless, the Trade Expansion Act went ahead and was followed by the Kennedy Round GATT negotiations – the sixth of a series of post-war conferences designed to cut tariffs and establish rules for international trade policies. By its own lights, the Kennedy Round was relatively successful; the weighted average of tariff cuts on industrial products was 25 per cent. But it left the Common

1. Quoted in Gerald M. Meier, *Problems of Trade Policy*, Oxford University Press, New York, 1973, p. 35.
2. On 6 December 1961, he said, 'I am not proposing, nor is it either necessary or desirable, that we join the Common Market; alter our concepts of political sovereignty, establish a "rich man's" trading community, abandon our most favoured nation treatment or create an Atlantic free trade area . . .' Quoted in John W. Evans's *The Kennedy Round in American Trade Policy: The twilight of the GATT*, Harvard University Press, Cambridge, Mass., 1971, p. 141.

Market intact – and if anything more cohesive than before, having negotiated with a 'single voice'. It did not succeed in eroding the two fundamental aspects of the Community – the Common External tariff (CXT) and the Common Agricultural Policy (CAP). And it left a sourness in Atlantic relations. For although the delegates had made a mammoth effort to reach final agreement, the talks had often been dogged by petty disputes which served to illuminate the degrees of transatlantic suspicion. Symbolic in this respect was the dispute over the American Selling Price (ASP). ASP is a standard of valuation, based on the domestic price of merchandise produced in the US, for calculating duties. It is applied to benzenoid chemicals, rubber foot-ware, canned clams, and cheap knitted gloves. Although benzenoid chemicals accounted for a relatively small share of total chemical trade, Britain and the EEC insisted that abolition of ASP be the condition for tariff cuts on chemical products generally. This required separate Congressional authorization which, in the event, Congress refused to provide.

The Kennedy Round tariff cuts came into effect too late to stem the flow of investment from the United States to Europe. By the time the negotiations were completed, the US trade surplus was slipping away and organized labour and domestically based industry were calling for protection against Japanese and European imports. In many areas, the Administration succumbed. Foreign exporters were asked to restrain 'voluntarily' the export of such products as textiles, beef, steel, etc. In this way, the Administration could head off protectionist legislation in Congress and disclaim any violation of GATT rules. Most of these restrictions affected Japan and Third World countries. But Europeans were affected by the restraint on exports of steel and steel products.[1]

1. The US Secretary of Commerce, Frederick Dent, justifies this restraint on the grounds that three-quarters of the steel industries in the world are either directly owned or indirectly supported by the government. 'The United States steel industry has suffered inadequate profit margins because of the political pricing of steel on a world-wide

In addition, the US has imposed its own restrictions on imports. Between 1962 and 1971, the number of US industrial imports subject to quantitative restriction, including 'voluntary restraint' rose from seven to sixty-seven, and, according to one expert, its 'restrictive impact is undoubtedly greater than the liberalizing effect of our tariff cuts in the Kennedy Round'.[1]

Nevertheless, the free trade ideology still runs deep. To the Administration, to the US multinationals, and the successful American farmer, protection is an admission of weakness – something to be equated, in an undertone, with isolationism. The US deficit, free traders will argue, was not due to a loss in the competitiveness of US goods, but to a rise in protectionism abroad. The elimination of barriers to US exports must be negotiated, according to the Chairman of the US Council of the International Chamber of Commerce, in order 'to buttress continued American leadership and achievement in the world economy'.[2]

The dollar crisis and the enlargement of the EEC provided the occasion for a new initiative in trade liberalization. Nineteen Seventy-Three was designated the Year of Europe. It was also the year when Nixon introduced a new Trade Reform Act in preparation for a new round of GATT talks, which the Administration attempted to dub the 'Nixon Round'. The bill gives the President powers to negotiate tariff cuts and to eliminate non-tariff barriers. But it also strengthens the safeguards against industrial dislocation caused by imports, and gives the President protectionist powers to use in the event of failure at GATT.

The issues have not changed; if anything, the

basis and it is essential if the United States is going to maintain a private steel industry that they [the steel companies] are encouraged to modernize and fulfil environmental requirements and expand to supply the needs of this country.' (Interview with *The Times*, 30 August 1973.)

1. C. Fred Bergsten, 'Crisis in US Trade Policy', *Foreign Affairs*, July 1971.

2. *Testimony on the Proposed Trade Reform Act of 1973*, Committee on Ways and Means, House of Representatives, 15 May 1973.

importance of trade barriers has lessened, partly because of
the internationalization of investment and partly because
industrial tariffs are, in any case, so low. As before, the
talks are really about the existence of the European Community itself. If the US succeeds in obtaining the desired
results, it will do so, at the expense of the present European
institutions. As before, US officials have made it plain that
it is not the European conception to which they object but
the present manifestations of Europe. Indeed, they suggest
that the current dispute would never have arisen had
Europe achieved political unity. According to George Ball,
the former Under-Secretary of State.

> It is not surprising . . . that doubts are being in-
> creasingly expressed at high levels of government as to
> whether the European Community will ever be more
> than a trading bloc, basically antipathetic to United
> States' interests.
> Because our commercial policy is now largely in
> the hands of the technicians it is no longer regarded bad
> form to speculate that America may have made a major
> error in encouraging the creation of the Community
> during the sixties, or even to suggest that we should
> shape our policies so as to try to weaken rather than
> strengthen the fabric of European unity.[1]

The four main issues before the GATT conference are about the identifying features of the European
Community. The first is the reduction of industrial tariffs,
which are now very low. There has been some talk of
eliminating them altogether, but this was rejected by the
Europeans on account of the political significance of the
Common External Tariff. Furthermore, it is argued that
any substantial reduction in tariff levels would lead to an
increase in non-tariff barriers which are much harder to
control. The Tokyo Declaration, approved by the parties
to GATT in September 1973, calls vaguely for 'negotia-

1. Speech at the Euro-American Conference, sponsored by
the International European Movement in Amsterdam, in March 1973.
(Quoted in *The Times*, 29 March 1973.)

tions on tariffs by employment of appropriate formulae of as general application as possible'.

More important are the negotiations on non-tariff barriers. In addition to quantitative restrictions, this term can apply to all manner of things – health and safety standards, labelling, taxation, etc. – which, intentionally or not, discriminate in favour of goods manufactured domestically. The ASP is one example. Another is the French decision to exclude imports of American poultry, on the grounds that hormones fed to American chickens could have a harmful effect on the fertility of Frenchmen. Yet another is the cost of applying US safety standards to European cars. The difficulty in negotiating about such barriers is very great; it is difficult to agree on what constitutes a non-tariff barrier, for one thing, and it is even harder to assess its effects, for another. Furthermore, many of the non-tariff barriers in Europe, about which Americans complain, are precisely those which contribute to the European institution. The Value Added Tax, for example, is not applicable to exports and hence is considered a hidden form of export subsidy; this is the one instance of 'fiscal harmonization' that Europeans can claim. In addition, so-called technological mercantilism is up for criticism. Europeans have consistently complained about 'Buy American' regulations in the field of defence procurement or in the construction of new urban transit systems for instance.[1] Americans have not been slow to respond with charges, for example, about 'Buy British' regulations in North Sea Oil and Gas drilling. One of the main props of the Europeanist case has been the need to cooperate on high technology projects in order to be able to compete more effectively with the United States. Since such projects – defence, space, nuclear energy – are government-spon-

1. In general, the Buy American Act requires that goods purchased by the US government be produced in the US unless the foreign-made product is between 6 per cent and 12 per cent cheaper. In the field of defence, the foreign products must be 50 per cent less expensive. Some foreign products may not be purchased at all, regardless of cost.

sored it is not surprising that the governments discriminate in favour of European contractors; indeed, this is a major element of the Commission's recommendations in these areas.

A third issue concerns the granting of generalized preference to developing countries. Again, this strikes at an essential feature of the European system – the free trading agreements signed with African and Mediterranean countries, with whom the Europeans have 'historic ties'. The US regards these agreements as vestiges of colonialism and a violation of the non-discrimination clause of GATT. Quite apart from the fact that many of the products exported to the Community by the associate members are competitive with similar American products – Florida citrus-growers claim to have been hit by the agreements – the Americans object to the principle of such agreements. According to the former US Secretary of Agriculture, Hardin:

> The European Community is now openly derisive of GATT–MFN requirements. The danger is that as a result of the present plans for enlarging the Community, European and African nations will have created a trading area sufficiently large to enable them to depart entirely from MFN treatment and will plunge the rest of the world into a trade jungle in which special deals become the practise rather than the exception, and in which spheres of trading influence will develop as a matter of course.[1]

Equally, Americans are concerned about the extension of European influence in the Third World – an influence which is not, as formerly, shared with the United States. George Ball attempted a masterly distinction between European and American forms of imperialism, by describing the latter as an open system. Such a system

would not, of course, preclude special bonds of friend-

1. Quoted in Richard N. Cooper, 'Trade Policy is Foreign Policy', *Foreign Policy*, no. 9, Winter 1972–3.

ship and intimacy between individual and developing countries, nor even some distribution of tasks among industrial nations on a geographical basis. But there is a major difference between ties based on cultural friendship or military necessity and ties predicated on special financial or commercial regimes that are discriminatory in character.[1]

The US, together with Canada, was initially unwilling to join the generalized preference scheme, initiated in 1970,[2] until such time as these special trade agreements were removed or at least modified. In particular, the issue revolved around the so-called reverse preferences, according to which the associated countries grant concessions to European exporters. The EEC Commission recently proposed a compromise whereby associate members are entitled to negotiate similar agreements with other countries – the US or Japan – thereby ending the preferential aspect.[3] It also announced that no new trade concessions would be made. The result is that the US has agreed to join the generalized preference scheme, but it has made exceptions for members of producer organizations such as OPEC. Since, as the next chapter argues, these organizations subsist on the alternative power of Europe and Japan, this measure is also directed against the European Community.

Subtract the Common External Tariff, fiscal harmonization, technological mercantilism, and associate trade agreements, and all that is left of the European framework is the Common Agricultural Policy. This is to be the fourth

1. Quoted in David P. Calleo and Benjamin M. Rowland, *America and the World Political Economy: Atlantic Dreams and National Realities*, Indiana University Press, Indiana, 1973, p. 235.

2. An UNCTAD Report on the generalized preference scheme shows that 'sensitive' products, such as textiles, footwear and agricultural products, amounting to 60 per cent of the goods imported from the Third World by the nations operating the scheme, are excluded. Further, as soon as a Third World country develops a successful export line, the tariff advantage is suspended.

3. Britain and its anglophone trading partners in Africa are quite ready to abandon reverse preferences.

issue at the trade talks, and numerous commentators have emphasized that it will be the 'touchstone' of the talks; the symbol of success or failure. Under the Common Agricultural Policy, the prices of European farm products are maintained at a sufficient level to guarantee the European farmer the equivalent of an industrial wage. (Actually, many Italian peasants remain extremely poor.) A variable levy is imposed on foreign farm products, based on the difference between the world price and the European price. Between 1963, when the Common Agricultural Policy came into effect, and 1972, EEC agricultural imports subject to the variable levy of CAP declined by one third. US agricultural exports to the EEC actually continued to rise, but only half as fast as US exports to the EEC as a whole. Moreover, American exports of products subject to the variable levy actually declined by 30 per cent between 1966 and 1971. Not surprisingly, when agricultural goods account for nearly a quarter of total US exports, there is a tendency to blame the Common Agricultural Policy for the trade deficit. The late Hubert Humphrey made public an internal Government Study which predicted that agricultural exports would total $8 billion in 1980 [1] if present protectionist policies remained in force, but would expand to $18 billion if protectionist barriers were dismantled. The equivalent figures for imports were $7 billion and $9 billion. And, according to a government report, published in 1971: 'The implementation of the Common Agricultural Policy by the European Community . . . was the principal obstacle to lowering agricultural trade barriers.' [2]

In his message to Congress about the Trade Bill, President Nixon said: 'One of our major objectives in the coming negotiations is to provide for expansion in agri-

1. Actually, this estimate seems very conservative, since agricultural exports in 1973 – admittedly a record high – totalled $18 billion, and, in 1975 $21 billion. This was up from $9·4 billion in 1972, and an average $6.7 billion over the previous five years.

2. 'United States International Economic Policy in an Interdependent World.' *Report to the President*, submitted by the Commission on International Trade and Investment Policy (*Williams Report*), Washington DC, G.P.O., 1971, p. 143.

cultural trade. The strength of American agriculture depends on the continued expansion of our world markets – especially for the major bulk commodities our farmers produce so efficiently.'[1]

The EEC have made it clear that the principle of the Common Agricultural Policy is not 'up for negotiation'. Yet it is difficult to see how the Europeans could guarantee an expanded market for US agricultural products and not change the principle, without, say, moving over from a system of price supports to a system of income supplements. It is, of course, possible that the issues will be transformed by a growing food shortage. An American embargo on soyabeans and soyabean cakes in July 1973, provoked a charge, by the European Commissioner for Agriculture, that Europe was being treated as a 'second class customer'.[2] The Americans responded by pointing to European embargoes on the export of wheat and rice. But the food problems of the last few years were not problems of shortage; they resulted primarily from changes in US agricultural policies, notably the reduction in grain reserves. If, as is probable, the US reverts to some system of world grain stockholding, world food prices will probably remain below European food prices.

Thus, the United States will only fulfil its objectives in the coming GATT negotiations if it also succeeds in dismantling the cherished policies which the Europeans have painstakingly agreed to share. This could occur either because the Community collapses or because greater European integration is achieved in which other policies matter more. In a more far-reaching European Community, the agricultural policy, for instance, would have much less significance; French farmers would be less powerful and other policies could fulfil the task of demonstrating the ability of Europeans to cooperate. It would be much easier

1. Quoted in *The Times*, 10 April 1973.
2. Soya accounts for one third of all protein in animal feed compounds in Britain and even more in Europe. Each year, Europe imports 8 million tons of soyabean and soyabean cakes, worth $100 million.

to go over to some other agricultural policy which allows for greater access by extra-European suppliers. Nevertheless, if it is to be effective, the European Community would have to pursue some policies which might be thought to constitute trade barriers. Quite apart from the likelihood of continued preference schemes with African and Mediterranean countries, of technological mercantilism, or VAT, the existence of an independent European entity is itself a barrier to free flows of goods, labour and capital. The stimulus, after all, to European integration is American parochialism. If the GATT negotiations succeed because European integration has increased, then the conflict will simply be shifted to a new arena – most probably an arena where the economic consequences of competition are more important – the control of investment, for example, or energy policy. They can only succeed in other words in a limited specific way.

If the GATT negotiations succeed through the collapse of the European Community – an unlikely eventuality – then, like the resurrection of a US-based monetary system, this must be viewed as part of the American reversion to international authority: a position maintained in a world of political conflict and economic stagnation largely through force.

On both sides of the Atlantic, dire warnings have been issued about the consequences of failure. In Germany the President of the Confederation of Industry has pointed out the risks of the formation of large inward-looking egoistic economic blocs, while Helmut Schmidt has suggested that 'if you retreat into blocs in these trade and monetary fields, then dramatic consequences must arise for foreign relations as a whole.'[1] American officials and commentators have been even more explicit: Peter G. Peterson, former Secretary of Commerce and US trade representative in Europe, told the Conference Board (representing American industry) in New York

The situation we face is one of exceptional chal-

1. Interview with *The Times*, 26 January 1973.

lenge. If we ignore it, we could drift further away from our European partners. The nature of this sort of drift is insidiously imperceptible. It is all too easy to arrive at an undesired destination without having noticed passing of telltale way stations.

Wars are rarely planned. Countries drift into them. Similarly, economic confrontations are rarely brought on by design. No one intended that the pair of wars in the 1930s take place, yet that happened and a devastating effect on world trade was not corrected until World War II.[1]

These warnings sound ominous precisely because they are made by spokesmen for government and industry, free traders fighting against a rising tide of protectionism, big business again protesting workers and small business. In a world of blocs, protectionism is bound to win out sooner or later because what economists call 'disequilibrium' is bound to develop. One bloc, whether it be America or Europe, will expand faster than the other. The slow-growing bloc is likely to take protectionist measures to avoid the unwelcome alternative of foreign deficit or unemployment. And the response to protection is protection. The free traders can only succeed through the disintegration of Europe and the reassertion of American power – something that becomes increasingly difficult as the American economy declines.

1. *US Information Service*, London, 22 January 1973.

6 Oil

The oil crisis of 1973 was perhaps the most important single event in reversing the trends of post-war economic development, exposing the differences within Western industrialized countries and slowing down world economic growth. The crisis was not, as is often supposed, an isolated chance occurrence – any more than were the crises about money and food. It was the culmination of a series of circumstances that originated in the mid 1950s and that paralleled developments in other economic spheres. In so far as the American government allowed it to happen, it can be viewed as one of a number of policies that included the rise in the price of food and the increase in arms sales that constituted the new parochialism.

'Survival of the fastest' is not simply a matter of market expansion. Capitalism absorbs increasing quantities of labour, food, raw materials of various kinds, and energy. Free traders have suggested that the GATT agenda should include the question of 'access to supplies'. The US Treasury Secretary Shultz asked Congress for 'unambiguous authority to withdraw the benefits of trade concessions to countries which impose illegal or unreasonable restraint on sales of materials in short supply'.[1] And in the 1975 Trade Act, Congress authorizes the Administration to withhold participation in the generalized preference scheme for underdeveloped countries from nations which belong to supplier organizations.

This concern about 'access to supplies' has nothing to do with shortage – raw materials are hardly more scarce than they were before the world wars when Germany and Japan expressed such anxieties. Rather, like the concern about 'free trade', it is a defence of the strong. It reflects the dominance of American corporations in the supply of raw materials and of American influence over supplier governments. And, like the American initiatives in trade negotiations, it is prompted by the erosion of this dominance. Through special bilateral deals with suppliers, dubbed 'protection' or 'supply mercantilism', other industrialized countries can arrange preferential terms for supplies, which are often associated with the penetration of American markets.

Scarcity panics about raw materials stem not so much from the prospect of absolute depletion as from domestic depletion. And even domestic depletion is a function of the dominant technology. Oil replaced coal as cars replaced trains. Technologies of the future may well be based on raw materials or new forms of energy in abundance in fast-growing industrial economies. It might be argued that an indicator of economic decline is increased dependence on imported supplies. The United States, for example, was traditionally renowned for its abundance of raw materials. Yet, of the thirteen basic raw materials needed for a modern economy, the US, in 1970, was dependent on imports for more than half its supplies of six. By 1985, it is projected to be dependent on imports for more than nine of the thirteen basic raw materials, including three major ones – bauxite, iron ore and tin.

The idea that underdeveloped countries might be tempted to conserve their rare supplies has raised the

1. Quoted in the *Guardian*, 4 March 1974.

spectre, handily substantiated by the oil crisis, of producer cartels coming together to bring about the downfall of the industrial world. Yet there is plenty of evidence, available at the highest levels of government, to suggest that the spectre is somewhat thin. An internal US State Department study, for example, concluded recently that countries exporting critical raw materials such as copper and bauxite might try to create a cartel to restrict production and raise prices, but they are unlikely to succeed. One reason is the potential for substitution. Copper can be replaced by refined aluminium, bauxite can be replaced by tin in making cans, cans can be replaced by plastic or glass containers, and so on. Despite warnings that 'the opportunities for substitution frequently insure that scarcity is contagious',[1] it is improbable that producers of raw materials and *all* their substitutes will restrict supplies simultaneously. Another reason why producer cartels may not succeed is the existence of stockpiles in rich countries, the potential for economizing in the use of materials, and the potential for accelerated recycling. The scrap ratio in aluminium, for example, could be increased from 17 per cent to nearly 45 per cent under an active recycling policy. Then there are likely to be alternative sources of supply. It is estimated that 40–45 per cent of all non-fuel mineral reserves are located in underdeveloped countries. A further 35 per cent is located in developed countries and 25–30 per cent in centrally planned economies. It is difficult to envisage cartels which can encompass Western industrialized nations, socialist countries as well as Third World countries.

But more important than any of these is the political and economic weakness of most supplier countries. Many of them are one-commodity economies; they lack the foreign exchange reserves to cushion the immediate impact of restrictions and are generally dependent on industrialized countries for vital supplies of capital equipment or even food. Others may have regimes whose existence depends on the goodwill of some rich country. The State Department

1. Lester R. Brown, 'The World Resources Shortage', *International Herald Tribune*, 26 November 1973.

study examined the case of copper producers, a group of relatively homogeneous underdeveloped countries producing a critical raw material. In 1967, Zambia, Zaire, Chile and Peru created a copper exporters' organization, CIPEC (Conseil Intergouvernemental de Pays Exportateurs de Cuivre). At the time Chile rejected a proposal for raising copper prices on the grounds that it would lead to world depression. Now, since the *coup*, Zambia has cut off relations with Chile. But, in any case, Zambia is unwilling to jeopardize relations with the US because it has just negotiated a $217 million long-term US Export–Import Bank loan for a hydroelectric dam and electric transmission lines. Other producers, the International Bauxite Association, for example, may go further but, in the end, they too are likely to repeat the long history of failure among producer cartels. 'Someone cheats; some outsider becomes too important to be ignored; the value of selling more becomes greater than that of holding the price line; prices are held too high to keep the market from shrinking; new producers appear; substitutes are developed; technology permits users to get more of the same quantity.'[1] In 1973, the US National Commission of Materials Policy concluded that no 'economic and political basis' exists for an effective cartel of raw materials producers in any commodity except petroleum.

It is difficult to believe that the concern about producer cartels is genuine. It is more likely to be an excuse – an excuse to exert pressures on supplier countries, through aid, through technology transfers, and, ultimately, through the threat of military intervention. And these pressures will be exerted not because resources are scarce, even though they may be, but because control over resources can bring substantial corporate advantages. So long as extraction, refining and distribution are in the hands of private companies, there will be no discrimination in supplies. Profit has no nationality and the company will

1. William Diebold, Jr, 'US Trade Policy: The New Political Dimension', *Foreign Affairs*, April 1974.

sell to the customer who pays most (although, of course, its home government may be able to enforce restrictions on the choice of customer). But the nationality of the company does matter when it comes to politics, prices and markets. A European government can break into American markets, or preserve its own, through making special arrangements for supplies on better terms than those offered by an American company. A favoured European ploy is participation in public mining or extraction enterprises – something which, until recently, has been anathema in the United States. An Italian company, for example, participates in the publicly owned Zambian copper mines; this is significant not so much because it secures supplies of copper to Italy but because participation has increased the ties between the Italian and Zambian governments and has opened new commercial outlets for Italy in Zambia. Italy is selling Zambia arms and cars and is building an oil refinery.

Much of the current emphasis on producer cartels arose from the oil crisis – a crisis which apparently represented a successful instance of supplier restrictions. Yet the Arab oil embargo succeeded, not because the oil producers are exceptionally rich and exceptionally cohesive, although they are, but because the embargo was not altogether unwelcome to American oil companies and to the American government. It provided an opportunity to underpin the American oil monopoly and to strengthen the dollar.

As with other supplies, no one, except the ecologists, is seriously worried about absolute depletion of the sources of energy. It is difficult to estimate the extent of the world's potential oil supplies because exploration has concentrated on politically 'safe' areas and because oil experts are mainly company spokesmen, with an interest in emphasizing oil scarcities. Nevertheless, it seems clear that, on the basis of known reserves, there will be no physical shortages before the year 2000, and that there may well be new discoveries in under-explored places like the continental shelf, particularly in the North Sea,[1] and the east coast

1. The Dutch Professor Peter Odell insists that discoveries of natural gas and oil in the North Sea are far larger than had been made

of America, and the west coast of Africa. And then there are other sources of energy: there is plenty of coal left under the ground, there is shale rock and tar sands, and there is nuclear energy. None of these sources is as desirable as Middle East oil. Underwater drilling is difficult and dangerous – spillages can kill marine life and pollute beaches; coal is expensive and mining is a most unpleasant job; shale rock and tar sands could ruin vast areas of natural beauty, like the Colorado mountains; nuclear energy carries with it awesome risks. The cheaper, cleaner sources of energy which may ultimately provide the answer – nuclear fusion or direct solar collection – will not be available soon.

But it is not the expense and pollution of future energy sources that governments are worrying about. Rather it is the prospect of domestic depletion. Before the Second World War, Europe and America were relatively self-sufficient in their energy requirements. Europe depended largely on coal and on gas derived from coal, with some countries, notably Italy and Scandinavia, using hydro-electric power. America used coal and oil, extracted from the American substructure. The discovery of cheap oil in the Middle East revolutionized the energy situation, making it less and less profitable to keep open mines and older oil wells. As of 1973 Western Europe depended on oil to meet 65 per cent of its energy requirements and, of this, 95 per cent was imported. Japan used oil to meet 75 per cent of its energy requirements and imported 99·7 per cent of its oil. The US, on the other hand, still supplied more than 70 per cent of its oil requirements. But this proportion was falling and before President Nixon launched Project Independence, to make America self-sufficient over the next decade, it was estimated that America would meet over half of its energy requirements through imported oil.

During the 1950s and 1960s, the oil business was a buyer's market. It was dominated by the seven big oil

public. The Groningen natural gas field, alone, is known to be the largest outside the Soviet Union.

companies – five American, one British, and one Anglo-Dutch – known as the 'international majors'.[1] These companies held the bulk of the oil concessions granted by producer countries for exploring, drilling and extracting, and they also controlled the business of refining and marketing. As late as 1968, the international majors were still responsible for 77·9 per cent of world production, 60·9 per cent of world refining and 55·6 per cent of world marketing facilities. Producing countries were dependent on the oil companies to provide them with the necessary technology and with the refining and market outlets. No one country could attempt to nationalize the oil companies operating on its territory or to withhold supplies in order to gain substantial price increases for fear of losing market opportunities. (This is, in fact, what happened to Mexico, which nationalized oil production in 1938.) Moreover, governments which attempted such a course tended to be overthrown. Hence Pérez Jiménez overthrew the Acción Democrática government in Venezuela after it had been elected to power on an oil nationalization pledge in 1948. Similarly, in 1953 the Shah of Iran, with help from the CIA and the US military mission, overthrew Dr Mussadeq, the popular Prime Minister who had attempted to nationalize the Anglo-Iranian oil company.[2]

The dominance of American oil companies was highly lucrative for the United States as a whole. As of July 1973, a barrel of crude oil, produced in the Persian Gulf, fetched $2·50. Of this, $1·60 went in taxes and royalties, 10 cents in production costs, and 80 cents in profit. Yet nearly every cent came back to the United States in one form or another. Thirty per cent of US

1. The companies are Standard Oil of New Jersey (Esso, Exxon, or Jersey), Standard Oil of California (SoCal or Chevron), Standard Oil of New York (Mobil), Texaco, Gulf Oil, Royal Dutch Shell, and British Petroleum (BP).
2. Not surprisingly, this manoeuvre enabled American companies to gain a foothold in Iran for the first time. Ironically, too, in view of the fact that the American role in Iran was justified by the granting of an oil concession to the Soviet Union, later withdrawn, during the post-war Soviet occupation of Iran.

overseas investments are in oil. Sixty per cent of American profits repatriated from Third World investments come from oil. And, in addition, Arab governments spend their revenue by buying American arms, American luxuries (it is Cadillacs and not Mercedes-Benz or Citroens that are abandoned in the desert), and through investing in American business.[1]

By the end of the 1960s, however, this situation was beginning to change. First of all, the dominance of the international majors was being eroded. From an early date, a number of domestic American oil companies began to seek low cost crude supplies abroad. The government reaction to increased oil imports was the imposition of quotas in 1959.[2] In consequence, the so-called 'newcomers' were forced to find alternative outlets for foreign crude oil and hence began to build up refineries and distribution networks overseas. Some of the newcomers were themselves vast companies deserving a place in *Fortune*'s list of the top 100 US companies.[3] In addition to these American companies, European firms began to bid their way into the business. Prominent among them were the Italian state holding company, ENI; the French companies, Compagnie Française des Pétroles and Elf/ERAP; and the Belgian Petrofina. More recently, Japan has been making its own arrangements for Middle East oil. And, finally, the producer countries themselves have set up companies – Iran's NIOC, Algeria's Sonatrach, and Saudi Arabia's Petromin. These companies still only account for a small share of the market, but they are said to have had a major effect in lowering the price of fuel among industrialized

1. Only Britain can claim similar advantages through its stake in BP and Shell and its historical hold on Arab leaders.
2. After protests from threatened domestic producers, the Eisenhower Administration called for voluntary restraint in importing in 1954 and 1958, using the 'security of supply' argument. As newcomers invaded the international oil fields, the majors joined domestic producers in calling for protection. In 1959, quotas were introduced which froze imports at roughly the share of total oil supplies in 1959.
3. They included, for example, Standard Oil of Indiana, Phillips Petroleum, Sun Oil, Marathon Oil, Continental Oil.

countries,[1] up to the end of the 1960s, and in reducing the dependence of producer countries on the international majors. Some of the newcomers offered special terms in order to break into the business. Companies like ENI, for example, were prepared to split profits with countries like Egypt or Algeria on a 25:75 basis instead of the 50:50 basis offered by the majors.

In recent years, Japan and the European governments have come to see the value of these special arrangements. Since 1965, the main target of Japan's oil policy has been 30 per cent 'yen crude' by 1985; 'yen crude' means home-produced oil or oil produced overseas by Japanese companies. In pursuit of this target, Japan has embarked on joint exploration and development efforts in Canada, Alaska, Australia, Abu Dhabi and the Sea of Japan. It has taken a share in the Nigerian State enterprise and gone into partnership with Mobil and the Iran State company. In Europe, France has been at the forefront of the oil offensive in words, although she has probably been matched by Germany and Italy in deeds. The French have emphasized that before Europe can formulate a common energy policy, the domestic commercial market must be controlled – implying that the dominance of American companies over European refineries and markets must be broken down. And a Euro-expert has pointed out that

> One of the objects of establishing a customs union embracing major European trading companies was to provide a counterpart to the economic strength of the United States. In these terms, it is clear that Europe needs to build up a substantial position with regard to energy supplies. In particular, this involves European companies taking an increasing share in the oil industry.[2]

This approach has been echoed in much of the

1. The price of fuel did not fall in the US, Britain and France. The US was protecting domestic oil, Britain was protecting coal and France was protecting Algerian oil.
2. Richard Bailey, *The European Community in the World*, Hutchinson, 1973, p. 145.

European press. Hence, a correspondent of the British *Sunday Times* writes:

> If we shake our minds clear of the inheritance of the past and accept that the balance of power has changed, it ought to be possible to begin constructing a series of special relationships with countries who have what we want to sell . . .
>
> But it should be clear, we want them as *our* partners, and would offer special deals with that in mind – the idea that we can achieve this end by cooperating with the Americans and Japanese is almost starry eyed. Europe is nearer than its industrial rivals to the oil reserves of the Middle East, and it is up to us to exploit this fact for our benefit rather than theirs.[1]

The second development in the international oil business was the coordination of producer countries' bargaining stance. Up to 1960 the companies were able to appropriate all the profits made from their foreign oil fields. The cost of production ranged from 10 cents in the Middle East to 50 cents in Venezuela, to three dollars in the US. Correspondingly, the post-tax rate of return on investment was around 70 per cent in the Persian Gulf, 20 per cent in Venezuela and 10 per cent in the US. As competition began to diminish the market price of oil, so the oil companies attempted to retain their profit margins by lowering posted prices – the fictional prices on which taxes were calculated. In response the producer countries – who were beginning to note the vast profits being made by others from their low cost oil – formed the Organization of Petroleum Exporting Countries (OPEC). Although OPEC succeeded in preventing a fall in posted prices, it did not achieve much in the way of positive measures during the 1960s. As late as 1966, the notorious Saudi Oil Minister, Sheikh Yamani, said that 'we don't believe the OPEC programme is a

1. Keith Richardson, *Sunday Times*, 27 May 1973. (Italics in the original.)

useful or workable instrument for strengthening prices'.[1] Yet after 1970, as a result of a series of agreements, revenues shot up from 47 cents a barrel in 1971 in the Persian Gulf, to $1·60 in the summer of 1973. And after the Middle East war, they rose even faster.

The producing countries were able to make these demands, partly because of the political changes induced by the oil industry itself. For one thing, the Middle East countries had more revenue than they could absorb. They were quite prepared to halt production until the oil companies gave in. It was increasingly coming to be realized that oil in the ground was a better investment than depreciating dollars. King Faisal of Saudia Arabia said: 'The Americans tell us that we can't drink our oil but have to sell it. My answer is, we can't eat dollars either.'[2]

For another, the oil industry had helped to create a vociferous nationalist urban class who saw no reason why the profits from oil should be appropriated by industrialized countries and who demanded an increasing anti-Western stance – and, among Arab countries, anti-Israel – from their governments. The power of these groups was demonstrated in the Libyan *coup* of 1969. Most important was the fact that the American ability to bring recalcitrant oil governments to heel was much diminished, in part by domestic politics and in part by the international challenge that could be posed to a brute demonstration of American power. Indeed, the growing independence of Europe and Japan provide alternative outlets for radical Arab leaders seeking to nationalize oil or to diversify sources for arms. Arab oil leaders have stressed the political and economic opportunities for cooperation now that they 'cannot rely on either of the two super powers'.[3]

But it can be argued that none of these factors was sufficient to create the kind of solid bargaining power that

1. Quoted in 'The Oil Fix: An Investigation into the Control and Costs of Energy', *Anti-Report*, no. 8, London 1974.
2. Quoted in *International Herald Tribune*, 12 September 1973.
3. Speech by Dr Nadim Pachachi, former Secretary-General of OPEC, 'The Future of Oil – an Arab View', September 1973.

was apparently exhibited after 1970. What changed the position of the OPEC countries was not so much their increasing independence as a growing realization in the United States that OPEC demands could be of parochial advantage. According to the *Economist*:

> No one outside the US administration can prove whether this suspicion (that agreements with the OPEC countries are the product of American corporate and government policy) is correct. It may be wholly incorrect. But even if it is, the fact that the suspicion exists inside the industry is significant, as is the guess, widespread in some places, as to at least one of the reasons for the administration's attitude. According to it, the Americans gave in to OPEC readily because they saw increased prices as a quick and easy way of slowing down the Japanese economy.[1]

The culmination of Arab pressure on oil companies was also the occasion for an American comeback. During the Yom Kippur war of 1973, the Arab oil exporters cut back production by 25 per cent and imposed total embargoes on supplies to the US and Holland. In March 1974, after the Golan Heights ceasefire, the embargo on the US was lifted, although production remained at 85 per cent of September 1973 levels.

The embargo affected the US much less than Europe and Japan. The US then took 6 per cent of its oil directly from the Middle East and 3 per cent, indirectly, via European refineries. (The shortfall in American oil in 1973 cannot be blamed on the Arabs; rather it was due to shortage of refining capacity as well as deliberate corporate policy.) The main effect of the embargo was not physical shortage but a rapid rise in price. This affected America much less than Europe. OECD predicted that in 1974 the increased cost of crude oil would impose a burden of $40 billion on the current account balances (trade and invisible earnings like shipping, tourism and repatriated profits) of industrialized countries. This burden would not be spread

1. *Economist*, 7 July 1973.

evenly but would be concentrated in those countries heavily dependent on imported oil. Britain would bear $10·5 billion, Japan and Italy would bear $8·5 billion each, and France would bear $6·5 billion. The American balance of payments, on current account, was expected to be in rough equilibrium. In fact, the fast-growing economies were able to offset their oil deficits with increased exports of manufactured goods. The main burden of the oil deficits in 1974 and 1975 was borne by underdeveloped countries, slow-growing European countries like Britain and Italy and developed primary producers like Australia and New Zealand.

The benefit to the US did not just stem from its independence from high import costs. Oil profits have greatly increased as well. Take Aramco, for example. Aramco is the consortium of Exxon, Texaco, SoCal, and Mobil, which operates in Saudi Arabia. In January 1973, Aramco's price for a barrel of crude oil was $2·40, and its margin, after taxes and royalties of $1·61, was 79 cents. In January 1974, Aramco's price had risen to $10·83 and its margin, after taxes and royalties of $7·10, was $3·73. Also high profits made on the production of oil enabled the major companies to narrow their margins on refining and distribution and squeeze out many of the independents. This was true in Europe as well as in America. Hence, it served to renew the monopoly of the international majors. (Also important, but incidental to this argument, was the fact that the crisis helped to overcome environmental objections to the development of alternative sources of energy.)

Finally, the crisis enabled the American government to play the part of the liberal world leader and enunciate the principle of free access to supplies. In the aftermath of crisis, most countries – some, like Britain and France, more noisily than others – have accelerated their efforts to arrange bilateral arms-for-oil or industrial supplies-for-oil deals. Dr Kissinger, although not averse to arranging such deals for the United States, described them as 'ruinous' and 'selfish' and took the initiative in arranging the coordination of energy consumers.[1] At an energy conference called in Washington in 1974, President Nixon warned the participants that go-it-alone policies would 'drive prices up, drive our economies down, and drive us all apart'. He said that

> having achieved peace in the sense of absence of war, we will not follow a generation plagued with war with a generation plagued with warfare . . .
>
> Each of us has the responsibility to look for the interests of its own country. But we can have no real security in the world unless we are all secure. We cannot have a new trading system where each tries to gain at the expense of others. The same is true in what negotiations we may engage in monetary affairs and I would say the same is true of energy.[2]

And Kissinger said that failure to resolve the energy crisis 'would threaten the world with a vicious cycle of competition, autarky, rivalry and depression such as led to the collapse of world order in the thirties'.[3]

These words had a familiar sound. Not surprisingly, the US found, at least temporary, support from the Atlanticists in Germany and Japan and from Britain, whose oil companies also stood to benefit from protection from bilateral deals. But the French, who called for a world energy conference, saw the conference merely as 'an attempt' in the words of Michel Jobert, then Foreign Minister, 'to get Europe (and Japan) back into the Atlantic system'[4] and argued that it 'could lead fatally to a confrontation or clash with the producer countries and perhaps with underdeveloped countries as well'.[5] His views were echoed by Arab spokesmen. Libyan radio described the Washington Conference as:

1. Quoted in the *Guardian*, 11 January 1974.
2. Quoted in *International Herald Tribune*, 13 February 1974.
3. Quoted in *International Herald Tribune*, 12 February 1974.
4. Quoted in the *Observer*, 17 February 1974.
5. Quoted in *International Herald Tribune*, 12 February 1974.

an aggressive act against the oil-producing states, particularly the Arab states.

It is an American trap to sanctify American tutelage in Europe, on the one hand, and to internationalize oil sources, by means of force, on the other.[1]

The Americans heve succeeded in establishing an International Energy Agency (IEA) and agreement has been reached about oil sharing among consumers in the event of another cut-off and about financial arrangements for coping with oil deficits. But there remains a fundamental ambivalance in the American position. Initially, the Americans gained the cooperation of the other consumers through the demand for an oil price reduction. A truly international authority, acting on behalf of world capitalism, would espouse such a policy at the expense of domestic American economic interests.

However, American attempts to reduce the price were not very wholehearted and more recently the American Administration has favoured a price floor to encourage investment in self-sufficiency. The Americans have persuaded the members of IEA to agree to a minimum safeguard price system, which is not the same as a price floor. The high price is essentially a parochial policy. It is the use of international authority, in the interests of the American balance of payments and the monopoly of the big US oil corporation and, as such, it is an unstable policy. For European nations or Japan are bound to resist American oil dominance and to develop new oil companies, which compete through price reductions and special bilateral deals. Indeed, this is the purpose of the European 'dialogue' with the Arabs, described by the *Wall Street Journal* as 'sycophantic'. The Prime Minister of Libya made it clear that the oil embargo on Europe would be lifted when 'Europe begins to send modern weapons to the Arabs and to cooperate with us technologically'.[2] And this of course is what the Europeans are doing, not only because oil is an

1. Quoted, ibid.
2. Quoted in the *Guardian*, 14 November 1973.

important commodity but also because oil is the key to the Arab market – a market for arms, capital equipment and consumer luxuries, a strategic outlet for further markets in the Far East and Africa, and a source of profits and investment funds. In this sense, oil is a major cause of conflict between Europe and America. In the sense that the Arab market is not one that can be lightly given up.

7 Defence

Potentially, the Western European nations possess all the attributes that are supposed to confer military might. Together they maintain as many troops as the United States. They possess a highly sophisticated armaments base, capable of producing intercontinental ballistic missiles, nuclear missile-firing submarines, and aircraft carriers (something the Soviet Union has only recently built). In some areas of weapons technology, for example anti-aircraft missile defences or vertical take-off aircraft, they are more advanced than either of the two super powers. They also supply large numbers of weapons to armed forces outside Europe. In 1975, the arms sales of Britain and France alone totalled more than $5 billion.

Yet European leaders, such as Michel Jobert, the former French Defence Minister, describe Europe as 'disarmed', and American leaders, like James Schlesinger, the former US Secretary of Defense, complain of the inadequacy of the European defence effort. This splendid military arsenal is fragmented under several different national commands, each of which is individually small. Schlesinger would like to see more of it integrated into the NATO structure, dominated by the United States, while Jobert would like to see it integrated into an independent European defence structure. President Ford has called upon the Western allies to become 'truly one in the allocation of defence tasks, support and production' so that the defence effort is 'more than the sum of individual parts'.[1] The Commission of the European Community has called for a European arms procurement agency in order to rationalize European defence and defence production.

This debate has acquired a new urgency with the new clamour about Soviet military spending. But, as in the 1940s, the clamour is more consequence than cause of the appeal for a common defence. Soviet military expansion has not accelerated; there has been no marked change in Soviet defence policy. The cumulative effect of Soviet military spending on the power balance between East and West is a matter of argument not fact – a matter of perception.

The picture that is widely presented in the media is very different from the picture presented by experts within the US government – the picture, for example, that the head of the Systems Analysis Office gave to McNamara in the early sixties[2] or that Professor Samuel Huntingdon recently gave to President Carter.[3] It all depends on how you count divisions, on the geographical areas that are chosen for comparison, the weight given to technical sophistication, the account taken of the border war with China or the prospects of rebellion among Eastern European colonies, the ways of estimating logistics and support,

1. Speech to NATO Council, 29 May 1975, *Keesings Contemporary Archives*, 23–29 June 1975.
2. For a description, see Alain Enthoven and Wayne Smith, op. cit.
3. See the *Presidental Review Memorandum* of 10 July 1977, prepared by Professor Samuel Huntingdon for President Carter, reported in the *New York Times*, 8 July 1977. See also the report by the US Joint Chiefs of Staff, released by Senator Proxmire, quoted in *International Herald Tribune*, 1 February 1977.

etc. It does not take much imagination to suppose that the picture presented in the Kremlin or Peking is different yet again.

The fact that the proponents of integration have accepted an alarmist picture of the East–West balance must be understood in terms of their own situations, in terms of the importance such perceptions play in the divisions and ties of the Atlantic alliance. The debate about integration is much easier to explain in its own terms, in terms of the divisions and the ties of the Atlantic Alliance. In one sense, defence is an industrial product like any other. Crises in the defence industry parallel crises in other spheres of production; industrial pressures are bringing about changes in defence policies and industrial structures are limiting the possible choices that can be made. But in another sense, defence is a very special kind of product; it is organized force. It represents power and, for this reason, decisions about defence have a very special political and ideological significance. The future of the Western defence industries is bound up in the future of NATO and the future of Europe but decisions about NATO and about European defence are political decisions about the future of nation states and national economies. The new emphasis on defence integration is at one and the same time a response to industrial problems in the military sector and a response to what President Ford described as the 'strains and difficulties of the Alliance' resulting from similar problems in other spheres and the 'need to preserve the quality and integrity of this Alliance on the basis of unqualified participation'.[1]

The Crisis of the Defence Industry

In the West, defence industries are much like any other. They operate on the principles of private enterprise and the fastest survive. But their markets are not like any other and are determined differently. The markets of defence companies are governments and the factors which influence demand

1. Speech to NATO Council op. cit.

have to do with power and politics, and a wider range of economic and social issues which affect the relations between states. The crisis of the defence industries is the crisis of reconciling their internal structure with their markets; how to make politics keep up with perpetual growth, how to employ industrial capacity which keeps on expanding.

The crisis originated in the Second World War,[1] when aerospace corporations, as well as naval shipyards, underwent an enormous expansion. Afterwards, military procurement was cut and thousands of workers were absorbed into the civilian sector, but the factories were not dismantled. In Britain, arms corporations were sustained by exports to Latin America, as well as to the former dependencies in the Middle East and Indian subcontinent. In America, aircraft corporations, radar corporations like Raytheon, or specialized naval shipyards were stripped to a core of technical facilities and highly skilled design and management teams, financed by their wartime profits. It was not a situation which could be maintained for long and already, in 1946, aircraft companies were calling for a policy of steady and continuous procurement to secure the maintenance of a military aircraft manufacturing capability.

Such a policy made its appearance even before NATO and the Korean war. Thereafter, the cold war, the competition between the Soviet Union and the United States, ensured the development of what is now known as the 'follow-on' system. As soon as work was completed on one weapon system, it began on another, which incorporated improved performance characteristics – more firepower, greater speed or mobility, better protection, or improved communications. The rationale for a new weapon was based on a 'worst case analysis', which went, roughly speaking, along the following lines: to be fully prepared, we must assume that anything we make, the enemy can also make, and anything the enemy can make, he will make and use against us, if given the opportunity. The attempt

1. For some countries, it can be dated even earlier, to the naval arms race before the First World War.

to develop new technologies in order to improve performance characteristics became a race between competing manufacturers. In any military contract, the future of a company was at stake, and so every company was forced to allocate increasing resources to the design of new weapon systems. In this way, the competition between armaments manufacturers reflected and reinforced the military competition between nations. Just as the procurement of a weapon could be made obsolescent by the introduction of a new weapon by an enemy or even an ally, so the development and production of weapons could be made obsolescent by the invention of a competitor. Industrial competition fuelled the development of military technology, which formed the basis for the permanent arms race.

The constant improvements in performance characteristics involved continual increases in the complexity of manufacture. More and more people were required to design, develop and produce an individual weapon system. This increased complexity was reflected in increased costs. As of 1970, fighter aircraft could cost anything between seven and 320 times as much as a Second World War fighter plane. In comparison, the cost of labour and raw materials in the aircraft sector had only risen threefold. The same kind of cost increase, reflecting the same kind of complexity, can be found across the whole gamut of weapons systems. In the United States, major rises in defence expenditure followed the introduction of new generations of armaments in the late 1940s and the late 1950s and now follow the decisions about new weapon systems taken in the late 1960s. And this, of course, does not include the space projects and so-called environmental projects – transport systems, artificial hearts, pollution surveillance and control, automated housing – which have been used to employ the manufacturing capacity of the armaments corporations. All this has meant that the continuous employment of capacity – plant, machinery and manpower needed to manufacture modern weapons – can only be justified by advances in military technology which also involves continuous expansion.

In Europe, only the British and Swedish armament industries survived the war. Elsewhere they were rebuilt, during the 1950s, with American help; it was part of the rearmament programme initiated in Europe after the outbreak of the Korean war. By the early 1960s the French airframe sector could compete with that in Britain, and missiles were not far behind. Germany managed to establish an internationally competitive position in the production of armoured vehicles, artillery and naval vessels, while Italy has become famous for its helicopters and light trainer/ground attack aircraft. Belgium has retained a leading position in the production of ordnance; Fabrique Nationale exports around 90 per cent of its production and its rifle has been adopted as the NATO standard. But its aircraft company, SABCA, like the Dutch company, Fokker, has been absorbed into the French and German aerospace sectors.[1]

These industries had to be able to compete with American manufacturers, in order to justify their existence. Governments could only defend the purchase of domestically produced weapons, if they were comparable in technological sophistication to those possessed by America and Russia. Further, as it later proved, exports played a vital role in utilizing capacity. The ambition of every European manufacturer was to capture some part of the vast American market.

So the military competition was extended to Europe. But European governments could not afford to finance it: available resources were simply too small. The United States government has only recently experienced similar difficulties. In a period of full employment, when the communist scare was declining, and when the cost of welfare programmes established immediately after the war was rising, it was impossible to raise military expenditure by an amount sufficient to ensure continuous employment –

1. Fokker was merged with the German company, VFW. SABCA is now jointly owned by Dassault-Breguet and VFW-Fokker. They are the first transnational aerospace companies.

and, by implication, expansion – of the manufacturing capacity of armament corporations.

Two kinds of solutions presented themselves. One was to find other sources of finance, to expand the market by finding new customers. European governments took active steps to promote the sale of arms to foreign armed forces and to encourage diversification into civil spheres of production (space and environmental projects were, for the most part, ruled out because, like defence, they were too expensive). The other was to narrow the range of weapons systems produced domestically. This meant that each country would produce only a few weapon systems, capable of competing with American counterparts, and would abandon attempts to compete over the whole range of military production.

Civil production never provided a serious solution to the overcapacity problem except in the less advanced sectors like vehicles, where the problem was least. In ship-building, it proved, for the most part, uneconomic to build merchant ships with facilities intended for the manufacture of naval vessels. And civil aircraft have required increasingly expensive government support, to help them overcome the advantages of their American competitors – a large home market and substantial military funds for research. Concorde, of course, is a prime example, developed at a cost to the British and French governments of more than $2·5 billion.

In contrast, reliance on exports has proved an important feature of European defence industries. Around 30 per cent of the British and French military output is intended for overseas customers and this proportion is even higher in the advanced aerospace sector. Britain still leads the world in the export of new naval vessels. And the French Mirage fighter is the front-line aircraft of Israel, South Africa, Switzerland, Peru and other air forces all over the world. Nevertheless, exports do not, except in isolated instances,[1] pay for the development of new weapon sys-

1. Both Israel and South Africa have financed the development of French missiles. In particular, Israel financed the development

tems. Continued domestic funding is necessary if corporations are to retain an internationally competitive position. Moreover, the demand for weapons in Third World countries, which make up the bulk of the British and French export market, is somewhat erratic and a drop in orders can result in untimely pressure on the defence budget.

After 1965, when America was preoccupied with Vietnam and when Third World countries established their 'third worldism', wars in India and Pakistan, the Middle East and Africa fuelled the demand for weapons and oil-rich monarchies in the Persian Gulf and military regimes in Latin America shored up their positions with shining aircraft and tanks from France, Italy and Germany, as well as Britain. These purchases enabled European governments to maintain constant defence budgets, in real terms, from 1965 to 1971 and, hence, to increase social spending. But, already, by the late 1960s, industrial spokesmen were warning that failure to increase domestic procurement could reduce the competitiveness of European armaments in the 1970s. The French association of aerospace manufacturers complained as early as 1968 that the fall in conventional procurement could 'bring disequilibrium to the activities of our firms and compromise the future of our industry at a time when several countries – Germany, Japan, Italy, and India – have decided to develop their aeronautical activities'.[1] Its British counterpart argued, in 1971, that: 'The industry can only maintain its role as an exporter in the short run if existing major projects are brought to full fruition and in the longer run if a decision is made to support new projects at the earliest possible moment.'[2] Despite the export boom in the aftermath of the oil crisis, the pressure of new military projects has caused European procurement budgets to rise. European governments can hardly afford

of a medium ballistic missile, which is said to be suitable for carrying nuclear warheads. Iran has also helped to finance the development of British and American weapon systems.

1. 'L'Industrie Aéronautique et Spatiale, 1967–8', USIS, Assemblée Générale Ordinaire, *Rapport du Bureau*, Paris, 1968.
2. *A future Plan for Britain's Aerospace Industry*, Society, of British Aerospace Companies, January 1972.

this and, together with industry, are seeking new solutions.

The alternative to expanding markets is to stem the expansion of capacity. This can be done by narrowing the range of weapon systems under development and production. If national self-sufficiency is to be retained, and this is, after all, the claimed objective of a domestic armaments base, then this will have consequences for military strategy. Certain military roles must be abandoned; others, like a long-range strategic nuclear role, can never be attempted. Still others must be adapted in such a way as to be performed by single multi-purpose weapons systems. These changes are rarely popular among military men and among their traditional suppliers. If different branches of the armed services are to agree on a common weapon system, they must also agree on a common set of performance characteristics, known as specifications. But companies tend to grow up around particular branches of the armed forces – thus, in France, Breguet was a naval company, while Dassault services the Air Force – and, very often, differences over specifications reflect differences in manufacturers' capabilities and strategic disagreements get translated into arguments about the distribution of contracts. To overcome these obstacles, it has proved necessary to make organizational changes which will break up long-established procurement relationships.

In the face of these difficulties, governments have taken an active role in the process of industrial reorganization. Today, no single European country can claim more than two major airframe companies and the only large aeroengine companies are Rolls-Royce of Britain, and SNECMA of France. In almost every case the government has had to intervene to bring about mergers. For example, the French government used its approval of an order for 100 Mirage F-1, fighter aircraft, as a lever to force serious negotiations between the two private airframe companies, Dassault and Breguet. In return for amalgamation, the new company, Dassault-Breguet, was granted exclusive rights to French fixed wing military airframe contracts.

Today, the process of domestic concentration has reached national limits. To narrow further the range of military projects, most governments have adopted the policy of transnational collaboration in the development and production of major weapon systems.

Transnational collaboration originated in the 1950s with a series of American weapons jointly produced under licence in Europe of which the most important was the Lockheed F-104 Starfighter.[1] This was the period when the American balance of payments moved into deficit and when military assistance to Europe was being replaced by the sale of arms. The projects were justified by the American argument, expecially after Sputnik, that the overall level of technology within the Alliance must be raised. But they can be treated as part of the American offensive, which included Kennedy's Declaration of Interdependence and the MLF, designed to limit the independence that might result from European recovery. If European defence industries were going to be rebuilt, then it was better that they be dependent on American know-how. Further, collaborative production of American-designed weapon systems limited the market for indigenous European competitors. It ensured at once a place for American industry in the European market and a say for the American government in European production. In addition, it was a contribution to the balance of payments. Hence, American firms were actively encouraged to participate in the development of a European armaments base.

Despite their size, the American projects only accounted for a small part of total European expenditure on armaments. They were ambitious in the sense that they all involved a large number of European countries, and they all succeeded in enlarging Europe's capacity to produce weapons. They were very costly – the European versions of the weapons were much more expensive in terms of unit costs than their American counterparts – and they left

---

1. There were also two indigenous European projects – the Fiat G-91 and the Breguet Atlantique – but they were not very successful.

behind them a considerable resentment against American dominance in Europe. This was, of course, particularly true for Britain and France, who were producing independently designed weapons which could perform equivalent functions. In the early 1960s, however, a new form of transnational collaboration made its appearance based on indigenous European designs, and by the mid 1970s this was to dominate the budget of nearly every West European country. By then it was realized that if European countries, and more particularly Britain and France, were to compete with the United States in the military industrial sectors, an enormous expansion of capacity was going to be necessary, with or without domestic rationalization. And it was also realized that neither country was going to be able to raise sufficient resources to finance this expansion of capacity, and that the military market was not sufficiently large to ensure that capacity, once expanded, would bə fully utilized. The solution was a sharing of capacity and a sharing of markets through common procurement and production. Numerous projects, in every sphere of weapons technology, were initiated in this period. Particularly important were the aerospace projects; for example, the Multi Role Combat Aircraft (MRCA) which is expected to undertake most of the front line combat functions of the British, German and Italian air forces in the next decade.

But transnational collaboration has not solved the problems of the European defence industries, although it may have mitigated them. The cost of transnational programmes tends to be much higher than purely national programmes, although the extent of these extra costs is difficult to estimate. A proponent of transnational collaboration, Henri Ziegler, President of Aérospatiale and French Chairman of the Concorde project, has estimated that the additional costs of cooperation can vary from 18 per cent to 50 per cent, the latter figure being the most common.

The increase in costs is partly due to the obvious problems of administration and transportation. But, more importantly, it is due to conflicts in national industrial interests. These conflicts are reflected in the difficulties of achieving common specification and the equitable but often inefficient work-sharing arrangements. As with the disagreements between different branches of the armed forces within one country, international disagreements over common specifications generally reflect differences in manufacturers' capabilities. They result in very complex weapon systems, designed to satisfy different interests, and in some cases, as with the Anglo-French Jaguar, in the joint development of widely differing configurations.

Complexity of design is also accompanied by increased complexity in the manufacturing process. This is due to the work-sharing arrangements. Work is distributed among different countries, not on the basis of industrial capability, but according to the financial contribution of respective governments, and the size of their orders for the final product. This has involved a considerable amount of duplication in development, as technology is transferred from the more advanced to the less advanced national industry, as well as separate final assembly lines in each country. Not only has this increased the cost of each individual weapon system, produced collaboratively, but, particularly at the production stage, it has involved an enormous expansion of capacity. A transnational project involving two partners, for example, will require two assembly lines and therefore twice the production capacity of a single national project.

The overall European capacity to develop and produce weapons has consequently increased greatly. But in the national context, the effect of cooperation on the growth of capacity has been varied. Britain, for example, has entirely abandoned unilateral attempts to develop and produce major military civil aircraft or space programmes. Moreover, international collaboration has replaced not one but several projects. In contrast, Germany has never developed and produced independent advanced technology projects, and international collaboration has led to a substantial increase in both development and production capacity.

The disadvantages of transnational collaboration

in its present form are becoming increasingly apparent. Among the more advanced sectors of Europe's defence industry there is concern lest the equitable sharing arrangements will involve the loss of their comparative advantage, the transfer of development capacity and markets from the more advanced to the less advanced partners. The distribution of contracts is not based on the comparative advantage of defence corporations, but on the bargaining abilities of national governments; this process militates against countries, like Britain, where the industry is relatively advanced and the government relatively weak. The British electronics industry, for example, feels that 'its interests have been sacrificed for the sake of firstly the aero-engine industry and secondly the airframe industry'.[1] At the same time, the advantages to governments from sharing development costs have largely been offset by the phenomenal rise in the cost of individual projects; while the failure to reduce the growth of production capacity has compounded the pressure to increase domestic procurement and exports.

Two solutions suggest themselves. One, proposed by the Americans, is known as the 'Two-Way Street'. The other is the creation of European multinational defence companies.

The Two-Way Street is supposed to involve national specialization rather than transnational collaboration. The idea is that defence companies based anywhere in the Atlantic area can compete for standardized NATO equipment contracts and production will be concentrated where it is most efficient. Europeans will buy from America and vice versa theoretically according to the rules of capitalist competition. The flaw in the idea is the nature of defence markets. In peace-time, military efficiency is a subjective concept, depending on the operating principles

1. Dr Bernard O'Kane, Chairman of Marconi-Elliott Avionic Systems Ltd, 'The Outlook for the Electronics Industry in Europe', paper presented to the Management Studies Group symposium on 'Problems and Opportunities for Aerospace and Allied Technology in Europe', Royal Aeronautical Society, London, 7 March 1973.

of different armed forces. A German-designed tank is most efficient for the German armed forces, just as only a British destroyer could meet the requirements of the British navy. If the Two-Way Street is going to work, NATO will have to formulate common specifications for military equipment, which will involve greater harmonization of operating principles and unified budgetary control – in other words, much closer integration of national armed forces. Since NATO is dominated by the United States, an American sits at the top of the integrated command structure, the Two-Way Street, if it is to work efficiently, is likely to be a One-Way Street – another way of saying 'Buy American'. Indeed, given the fact that American arms companies are beginning to face the same problems as their European counterparts and, since the oil crisis, have become increasingly dependent upon burgeoning arms sales, this prospect is openly anticipated. Certainly, the Pentagon assumes that 'our NATO Allies will wish to depend more on US aircraft design and development.'[1]

The 'arms deal of the century' in which Belgium, Denmark, the Netherlands and Norway decided to buy the American F-16 fighter, with the maximum of political pressure and private corruption, is the first example. The American decision to buy an American tank and not the German Leopard may well be another.

The European alternative to the Two-Way Street, much favoured by the European Commission, is the truly European arms manufacturer. Such a giant firm would bid for new contracts and apportion work according to its cost-minimizing interest rather than to the national interest in maintaining or establishing certain types of capacity. This would lead to national specialization, concentrating work in those areas which are most efficient, benefiting the more advanced sectors of the industry and, through the avoidance of duplication, enable a reduction in the growth of both development and production capacity.

1. *Annual Defence Department Report* FY1977, Section IV/C/3/G.

The most enthusiastic proponents of this proposal are those firms which at present enjoy a comparative advantage and the governments which are experiencing the most severe constraints on military expenditure. On the government side it has been British Conservative leaders who have called for the formation of transnational European companies in advanced technology sectors. And on the industry side, Rolls-Royce and Dassault-Breguet have been at the forefront of demands for a unified European industry. Dassault-Breguet can be said to be the last European aircraft company independently developing a major combat aircraft and any consolidation of Europe's airframe industry is likely to be concentrated around this company. Similarly, Rolls Royce would hold a pivotal position in the formation of a multinational aero-engine company. Panavia, the consortium of firms established to administer the MRCA project, announced in 1970 a plan to produce an advanced strike/trainer aircraft as a private venture. In announcing the plan, the top Panavia executives made it clear that this was seen as an important step towards European integration in aerospace. According to Bölkow, Deputy Chairman of Panavia and head of the German company Messerschmitt-Bölkow-Blohm:

> We are moving towards fewer but stronger aerospace groups in Europe. These will be formed through the initiative of the leading aerospace companies and will have a truly European basis.
>
> The results of this trend should be increased efficiency, an improved competitive position in the world market and a much better ability to handle all programmes in Europe.[1]

But like the Two-Way Street, the creation of European multinational companies would mean greater military integration. Otherwise, governments might support the less advanced national defence companies, in the interests of national self-sufficiency and domestic harmony,

1. Press release, Panavia Aircraft GmbH, Munich, 9 September 1970.

and even deep-seated military traditions. When industrial reorganization took place within the national context, ministries of defence were able to impose a solution to the conflicts between different branches of the armed services, and hence create the conditions for a new set of military–industrial alliances. If the same kind of solution is to be found in the transnational context, where the conflicts are much more acute, a common European procurement agency will have to be established, with the authority to take procurement decisions on behalf of all European armed forces.

Such decisions could not be easily taken unless there were an integrated command and a common defence budget. An integrated command would be necessary to establish a set of criteria on which to base procurement decisons. Substantial agreement would have to be reached on the kinds of military tasks to be performed, the priorities for different military tasks, and the most appropriate weapons to carry out those tasks. A procurement agency could not take decisions about weapons, if substantial disagreement about overall strategy persisted. Equally, it could not take such decisions unless it was assured of budgetary control. Financial contributions to the development of new weapons systems could hardly be based on workshares in the absence of national companies, but if they were based on the size of national orders, governments could always refuse to contribute to projects of which they disapproved. Indeed, so long as national governments retain budgetary control, finance can always be used as a bargaining lever, and, unless some governments were prepared to sacrifice their national interests, the agency could degenerate into a mechanism for distributing national orders.

In other words, European arms companies imply European defence just as the Two-Way Street implies NATO and American defence. The crisis in Western defence industries has propelled government towards this choice but the outcome of the choice depends on a whole range of other issues; the implications for NATO and the integrated command system, the status of the Soviet military threat and the progress towards European unity. These issues have been discussed for many years. But it is only recently with the new expensive generation of 1970s weapons and the new-found American dependence on arms sales that they have become the anxious subject of industries and governments caught in the contradictions created by over-capacity in the sphere of military production.

The Crisis in Defence Policies

The debate about defence production has its counterpart in the debate about defence policies. The Two-Way Street is part of the new American emphasis on the importance of Atlantic cohesion and unity, in response to distressing tendencies of division and fragmentation. European collaboration is often viewed as a critical element in the creation of a European union with a single European defence policy.

As we have already argued, the case for Atlantic unity must be judged not against the Soviet threat but in terms of the conflicts within the Alliance itself. When NATO was formed in 1949, the overt threat of Soviet aggression was considered to be small and the proposals for upgrading European defence were minimal. NATO followed the Marshall Aid Plan and its main function could be said to be coercive, to hold the West together against the emergence of independent power centres – the possible consequence of economic recovery. When military aid to Europe was proposed, the purposes, according to a memorandum circulated throughout the US State Department, were 'to build up our own military industry', 'to create a common defence frontier in Western Europe' through the pooling of 'industrial and manpower resources' and 'particularly to subordinate nationalistic tendencies'.[1]

In a general psychological sense, NATO could fulfil these functions simply by its existence, by open and personal contact between governments, by the evocation

1. Quoted in Lafeber, *America, Russia and the Cold War, 1945-71*, p. 79.

of a common external menace. But there were two concrete mechanisms which brought the NATO countries more closely together and which established American authority. One was the integrated command system and the other was the active presence of American troops in Europe.

The North Atlantic Treaty contained no automatic and specific obligation to use armed force as a means of giving aid in the event of attack. Instead an elaborate system of integrated commands was established.[1] This system had the dual advantage of a concerted Western defence and of placing large sections of the European armed forces under the command of an American, in the form of the Supreme Allied Commander Europe, SACEUR. Theoretically, the command system comes into effect only in crisis, but, in practice, it involves a considerable degree of peace-time cooperation in tactical planning, training, etc. Even today, many Italians believe that no left-wing government could ever be formed in Italy because it would be overthrown by an American-backed military *coup*. And some people argue that this is precisely what occurred in Greece, in April 1967.

Nevertheless, outside NATO, national commands like national currencies were re-established. Indeed, so long as Britain and the United States insisted on retaining their national sovereignty, other NATO members could hardly be expected not to do the same. A solution to this difficulty was the European Defence Community, from which Britain and, of course, America excluded themselves, although it remained firmly pinned to the NATO framework. The EDC provided a mechanism for rearming Germany and, hence, adding to the strength of the Western defence. It ensured the division of Germany and hence the political orientation of foreseeable West German governments. And it guaranteed that German military might, supported by the Benelux countries, could always counterbalance the

1. The Brussels Treaty also established a nucleus land, air and sea command. But when it was signed in 1948, it was primarily directed against 'the renewal by Germany of a policy of aggression'. Later, it was incorporated into NATO.

potential dangers of leftist governments in France and Italy. Just in case national branches of the European armed forces might be tempted to secede, the EDC Treaty provided for integration down to the smallest military unit. (Even the integration of the British armed forces did not achieve this – regiments retain their Irish, Scots or Welsh characteristics.) The EDC Treaty was defeated by the French left. That it was the degree of supra-nationality implied by such tight integration to which they objected is indicated by the ease with which the Western European Union (WEU) was established immediately afterwards. WEU incorporated all the features of the EDC, including German rearmament, but it did not involve the same degree of integration.

The American interest in integration was revitalized by the formation of the European Community and the spread of non-alignment in the Third World. It was associated with the growth of the European defence industries, the MLF proposals, and all the other early signs of American parochialism. From the end of the 1950s, the US Administration constantly urged Europeans to increase their conventional commitment to NATO. The argument was that the strategy of flexible response, involving reduced reliance on nuclear weapons, introduced by the Kennedy Administration, and later the advent of 'nuclear parity', required increased conventional forces and that, as European countries became richer, they should carry a larger share of the military burden. The implication was that more troops should be committed to an American command and fewer to independent national commands.

This argument has been put more forcefully as signs of disintegration within NATO grow. On the one hand, there is, as described below, the development of a European caucus. On the other, there is what President Ford describes as the tendency for 'partial membership or special arrangements'. De Gaulle set the precedent when he argued that as Europeans established their economic independence they could no longer rely on the American commitment. He proposed that the French nuclear deterrent be operated on behalf of Europe and even, at one point, invited Chancellor Adenauer to pay for it. He also drew the distinction between the integrated command system, NATO, and the Atlantic Alliance and withdrew French forces from the former. After the Cyprus crisis of 1974, Greece took a similar step, while the commitment of the new Portuguese government to NATO has been less than enthusiastic. It is no wonder that, in these circumstances, the Soviet threat looms larger and the appeal for military integration grows more intense.

At the apex of the integrated command system are the American troops in Europe. Currently, the US stations 300,000 troops in Europe. The purpose of these forces is seen not only in terms of their direct contribution to the conventional defence of Western Europe – the European members of NATO have, after all, 2·7 million men under arms – but in terms of a visible American commitment. The presence of these troops is supposed to make credible the US nuclear deterrent to a Soviet attack on Europe and to provide, in Schlesinger's words, the 'psychological, political and military support . . . essential to the cohesion of this alliance of smaller states faced with the Soviet Union'.[1]

The emphasis is on the word 'cohesion' and so long as West European governments favour Atlantic cohesion, because they favour stability more than independence, the US troops will not be treated as an occupation force and will be welcomed.

As the United States began to use its international authority for parochial purposes, so it has been argued that the Europeans should pay for the privilege of the integrated command system. In particular, the presence of US troops has been used as a lever to exact economic concessions. In 1973, the annual operating costs of the troops were $4 billion, and the direct balance of payments burden was $1·5 billion. But it was estimated that the total sum devoted

1. *US troops in Europe*, Hearings, Subcommittee on Arms Control, International Law and Organization, Committee on Foreign Relations, US Senate, 25 and 27 July 1973, p. 72.

by the United States, in terms of weapons, reinforcements, logistics, and so on, to the defence of Europe was at least $30 billion.[1] This was equivalent to the entire defence expenditures of the Western European members of NATO.

In the early 1970s, it was being widely argued that Europe is a 'lounge lizard under an expensive American nuclear umbrella',[2] and that if the Europeans insist on being protected by America, they must pay their fair share of the costs – not in the form of direct payments because that would give the US soldiers the taint of being mercenaries, but in the form of trade concessions or purchases of American armaments. This argument acquired renewed force with the increasing success (up to 1974) of the annual Mansfield amendment on the reduction of US troops based abroad, and the 1973 Jackson–Nunn amendment to the defence budget which requires a 100 per cent offset in purchases of American goods or securities by Europeans to cover the cost of US troops.

This argument is not couched in terms of American self-interest. Quite the contrary, Americans have followed Dr Kissinger's lead in emphasizing Europe's narrow 'regional interests' and America's 'global responsibilities'. It is suggested that Europe is somewhat greedy and ungrateful, enjoying the benefits of being both an affluent trade rival and a dependent ally. This view was propounded at length by former Treasury Secretary Conally, in a speech to the American Bankers' Association:

We today spend nearly 9 per cent of our gross national product on defense – nearly five billion dollars of that overseas, much of it in Western Europe and Japan. Financing a military shield is part of the burden of leadership, the responsibility cannot and should not be cast off. But 25 years after World War II legitimate questions arise over how the cost of those responsibili-

1. *The Defense Monitor*, vol. 2, no. 5, 12 December 1973.
2. Joseph Godson, 'The Necessary Army', *Observer*, 8 April 1973.

ties should be allocated among the free world allies who benefit from that shield. The nations of Western Europe and Japan are again strong and vigorous and their capacities to contribute have vastly increased . . .

A second area where action is plainly overdue lies in trading arrangements. The comfortable assumption that the United States should – in the broader political interests of the free world – be willing to bear disproportionate economic costs does not fit the facts of today.

I do not for a moment question the worth of a self-confident, cohesive Common Market, a strong Japan, and a progressing Canada, to the peace and prosperity of the free world.

The question is only – but the 'only' is important – whether these nations, now more than amply supplied with reserves as well as with productive power should not now be called upon for fresh initiative in opening their markets to the products of others.[1]

In the early 1970s, American officials stressed that negotiations between Europe and America must cover the whole gamut of issues – commercial, financial and military. Implicit in such statements was the suggestion that if Europe were not amenable to American demands, US troops would be withdrawn from Europe. In March 1974, Kissinger suggested that the US troop commitment to Europe could be 'adjusted' if cooperation continued to erode.

Like other parochial policies, this 'blackmail', as the French Gaullist Debré described it, may improve the American economic position in the short run but provoke independence in the long run.

Advocates of an internationalist foreign policy, like many in the Carter Administration, have recognized the dangers. Paul C. Warnke, head of the US Arms Control and Disarmament Agency, has argued that NATO is

1. Quoted in Sweezy and Magdoff, 'The Dynamics of US Capitalism', *Monthly Review Press*, New York, 1972, p. 208.

too expensive and too dangerous to retain as a tool for the exaction of economic concessions.

Were we to seek to coerce compliance with our political and economic views by threatening the withdrawal of our defence support, our allies might well conclude that the support isn't worth much.[1]

President Carter has emphasized the American interest in Europe.

Indeed, the most important effect of the American troop debate may well prove to be the increased respectability of the case for a European defence. Raymond Aron has argued that the continued US presence 'psychologically weakens and discourages the Europeans from taking charge of their own defence',[2] while two defence experts have suggested that the withdrawal of US troops might 'precipitate a radical reshaping of the defence efforts of West Europeans, including the French'.[3]

It is no longer unorthodox to hint that America is, in some sense, less reliable than in the past. At a not too distant date, America might well withdraw her forces from Europe, either unilaterally when the annual Mansfield resolution is finally passed, or bilaterally through agreement with the Soviet Union. And as a result of détente 'we may conclude', according to Lord Chalfont, former British Minister for Disarmament, 'with some justification, that unless there is an unlikely and irretrievable breakdown in the talks (SALT), the territorial integrity of central Europe will no longer necessarily be regarded by either the Soviet Union or the United States as a nucleur *casus belli*'.[4]

In response to this new situation greater European integration of conventional forces is advocated. It has long

1. Quoted in *International Herald Tribune*, 19 March 1974.
2. Quoted in James Goldsborough, 'The Case For Reducing US Forces in Europe', *International Herald Tribune*, 12 April 1973.
3. Sir Bernard Burrows and Christopher Irwin, *The Security of Western Europe: Towards a Common Defence Policy*, Charles Knight & Co., London, 1972.
4. Lord Chalfont, 'Defending Europe,' *New Europe*, May 1972.

been held, probably wrongly, in Europe, that the Warsaw Pact enjoys a substantial conventional superiority in the central region of Europe and that only the US nuclear deterrent stands between Western Europe and Soviet invasion. The British and French nuclear forces are not generally considered adequate to deter a Soviet attack and, in any case, the British deterrent is not truly independent. The alternative is conventional defence or deterrence.[1] Since an increase in conventional forces would be costly and unpopular, the military efficiency of present forces must be increased through the integration of separate national commands and the rationalization of military tasks. 'The time has come,' writes an eminent German thinker, 'to create a stronger European identity within the Atlantic Alliance and to make Europe's contribution not the sum of efforts by various states but a joint undertaking.'[2]

A tougher version of this argument holds that the super powers have not just forgotten about Europe's interests; they might actually harm them. Some even suspect that the Soviet Union and America might combine to prevent the emergence of a powerful European entity. Perhaps this is what M. Jobert is worrying about when he emphasizes the need for a joint European defence effort. After the Middle East crisis of 1973, he said:

Experience has shown us that this super power tête a tête can just as easily lead to confrontation as to détente . . . these observations may be brutal but we must be realistic and lucid. They reinforce our conviction that if we want to stay free, have any influence in the world, participate in the determination of our destiny, then we must tirelessly pursue both European construction and our defense effort.[3]

1. There is an intermediate stage, involving the use of tactical nuclear weapons. Currently, however, their status and the strategic doctrine governing their use is unclear.
2. Karl Kaiser, *Europe and the United States, The Future of the Relationship,* Columbia Books, Inc., 1973, p. 117.
3. Quoted in James Goldsborough, 'France, the European Crisis and the Alliance, *Foreign Affairs,* April 1974.

Proponents of this view would like to see an independent European nuclear force, as well as an integrated conventional defence effort. Both Mr Heath, former British Prime Minister, and Herr Strauss, former West German Defence Minister, have proposed that the British and French deterrents be held in trust for all of Europe. Since the British deterrent is based on Anglo-American nuclear exchange and on American missiles and submarines, an Anglo-French *force de frappe* would mean British readiness to give away American nuclear secrets. This is unlikely to happen so long as NATO continues to function.

Most European leaders, except the French, emphasize that military integration should take place within the NATO framework. They have directed their efforts towards Eurogroup, a kind of caucus of European NATO defence ministers.[1] It is increasingly recognized, however, that Eurogroup cannot form the basis for an integrated European defence system. This is mainly because its membership does not correspond with the membership of the European Community. It includes Greece and Turkey – and also Norway. It excludes France and Ireland. Recently, the Commission of the European Community has proposed greater defence integration within the Community framework, while the French, who tend to oppose excessive integration, have proposed the WEU as the forum for a European defence policy. In 1976, an independent organization known as the European Programme Group was established. It includes France and aims to achieve European arms cooperation as well as participation in a genuine Two-Way Street and truly internationalist alliance. Some people suggest that this could mark a

---

1. In addition to studying the various ways in which they could extend their military collaboration – joint military training, personnel exchanges, joint support functions, and so on – and establishing a set of general principles for military collaboration, the members of Eurogroup have reassured the United States of their loyalty, through increasing their individual and joint commitments to NATO – albeit in rather small measure.

significant shift in the history of European defence cooperation.[1]

This is the background to the new American emphasis on standardization, communication and coordination within NATO and to renewed American promises about the commitment to European defence. A NATO report in 1973 called for integration on a NATO-wide basis and the Secretary-General of NATO, Dr Joseph Luns, deplored the fact that 'our constant need to remain ahead of our foes has been paralleled by a desire to get ahead of our friends.' He added, presciently, that the 'free enterprise system encourages such things'.[2]

The case for NATO integration and the case for European integration are both based on similar assumptions about the nature of the Soviet threat and the means for countering it. The differences in the two arguments are based on differing assumptions about American behaviour. The NATO case assumes an internationalist America, in which American money and American men and American arms uphold the Western defence system and the underlying cohesion of Western economy and society. The European case assumes American parochialism and that economic difficulties reduce America's dependability. Taken to its logical conclusion, this assumption has frightening implications. It does not only imply that America and Europe have divergent interests but also that the interests of one may threaten the other. It implies an intensification of competition between European and American arms industries which would contribute to wider conflicts of interest. It implies that Europe will have independent military backing in her political and economic differences with America and that the most important tool possessed by America to overcome disintegration and disunity is eliminated. If America no longer considered that Europe

1. D. C. R. Heyhoe, 'The Alliance and Europe: Part VI The European Programme Group'. *Adelphi Paper* no. 129 IISS, London, Winter 1976/77.

2. NATO Press Service, 28 September 1972.

was worth defending, that the cause of Western internationalism cost too much, it could only be because competition between the blocs was fully developed. The situation in which America actually failed to respond to Soviet nuclear blackmail over Europe could only be one of open discord. The compromise of European integration within NATO ignores the realities; like the Atlanticist conception of Europe, it attempts to evade the stark choice between American hegemony and Atlantic conflict.

The new urgency in arguments about NATO versus Europe stems from the crisis in the defence industry. The crisis has reached the point at which decisions are going to have to be made about the future direction of defence policies. Unless there are major changes in the social organization of defence and the defence industries, European nations face the choice of scaled-down national defence industries, with increased American imports, or expanded multinational defence companies. The former implies a reassertion of American authority, a future for American defence companies, and an increased financial burden on American taxpayers. The latter implies important political decisions about the future of Europe. If Europe is to be unified, its armed forces must be integrated: to overcome internal threats to unity consequent upon the economic and social dislocation caused by political integration and to provide military backing for its new-found global status as a super nation. The former British Defence Secretary, Lord Carrington, has written:

> Looking further ahead, I believe that Europe is going to emerge as one of the largest and richest communities in the world with the potential of the present super powers and it is unthinkable that this new Europe should lack adequate means of self-defence . . .
>
> Moreover, this new Europe will be a global power whether she likes it or not. Trade will be her life blood as it has been Britain's for centuries. Her interests will not stop at the Tropic of Cancer. Increasingly, West Europeans will have to look outwards and play

their part in maintaining peace and stability in the world.[1]

In so many words, Lord Carrington was expressing his conviction that Europe will become an imperialist power, with all the trappings that are required to withstand the competition from other imperialist powers. And although his Atlanticist sentiments may belie it, the competition for which those trappings are required is the competition from America. Competition from the Soviet Union can be withstood jointly. If Europe needs independent armed forces, it can only be because it needs military backing for policies in which the interests of Europe might clash with those of America.

1. Lord Carrington, 'The Future of European Defence', *New Europe*, November 1972.

8 The Third World

Perhaps the most important crisis in Atlantic relations was the Middle East crisis of October 1973. During the Yom Kippur war, West Germany imposed a ban on the export of US military equipment from US bases in Germany, via Israeli ships, to Israel – an action which prompted the Secretary of Defense, Schlesinger, to threaten a review of American military and diplomatic commitments to Germany. Britain imposed an arms embargo on all sides. And all European members of NATO, except Portugal, reportedly refused to allow landing rights to American planes airlifting arms to Israel.[1] According to a State Department spokesman:

> We were in a very critical period, a period which in many ways affected all of us – ourselves and our allies

1. Reportedly, the then Prime Minister Heath personally approved operations from Britain of the secret American SR-71 reconnaissance plane during the Yom Kippur war, provided the approval was not made public. Kissinger turned down the offer. Subsequently, Britain refused to allow American use of the RAF base at Akrotiri in Cyprus.

in Western Europe, and we were struck by a number of our allies going to some lengths to separate themselves publicly from us. It raised questions as to how that action squared with what the Europeans have often referred to as indivisibility on the question of security.[1]

Both Nixon and Kissinger made even stronger statements. Kissinger described the European behaviour as 'craven', 'contemptible', 'pernicious', and 'jackal-like'.[2] He was overheard to say, 'I don't care what happens to NATO, I'm so disgusted,' while a European parliamentarian reported after an audience that 'he delivered a tirade of the kind I have never heard in my whole experience of international negotiations.'[3] He charged the Europeans with regional self-interest, arguing that their support for the Arabs was dictated by oil, while American support for Israel arose from political morality.

The Europeans were equally annoyed. The United States had failed to consult them about the nuclear alert and had negotiated with Russia above their heads. It was hinted, moreover, that Nixon had flirted with millions of lives for domestic political advantage. Foreign Minister Jobert told the French National Assembly that the super powers had reduced the Common Market to impotence.[4] And in a speech to the Western European Union, he called on Europeans to realize their 'worldwide vocation' and reject the threat of 'imperious arbitrage' by the United States and the Soviet Union.[5] And, on this occasion, his words were echoed by the usually more Atlanticist Chancellor Brandt: 'In a world whose destiny can not and should not be determined by two super powers alone, the influence of a United Europe has become indispensable.'[6] And he

1. *Guardian*, 27 October 1973.
2. Quoted in Theodore Draper, 'Detente', *Commentary*, June 1974.
3. *Guardian*, 1 November 1973.
4. *International Herald Tribune*, 13 November 1973.
5. *The Times*, 23 November 1973.
6. Quoted in James R. Goldsborough, 'France, the European Crisis and the Alliance'.

also said that: 'Europe has become self-confident and independent enough to regard itself as an equal partner in this (Atlantic) relationship and it is as such that it must be accepted. *Partnership cannot mean subordination.*'[1]

It is no accident that the first occasion for Euro-American confrontation arose in the Third World. The slowdown in world economic growth, the intensity of industrial rivalry and the decline of American power has at once increased the importance of the Third World and blurred the boundaries of spheres of influence. States in pursuit of parochial interests can no longer afford to neglect the marginal markets; issues like the price of food and oil, which fundamentally affect Third World economies, become tools in what Chancellor Schmidt has described as the 'struggle for the world product'; the decline in US aid and overseas military spending increases the possibilities for independent action on the part of Third World governments, as does the growing importance of Europe and Japan as alternative sources for arms, technology, etc. All this contributes to the new debate about International Economic Order, to the solidarity of the 'Group of 77' (the underdeveloped countries in the United Nations) and to the new talk about a North–South dialogue. It is also the reason for increased tension in the Third World, for the multiplication of *coups*, wars and revolution.

It is in the Third World, moreover, at the edge of the main arena of confrontation, that economic disputes are first transformed into political issues. The governments of rich countries penetrate the Third World through support for particular political groups – often those that are sympathetic in outlook – and as the relationship hardens, they are drawn into local power struggles which, in turn, may evolve into the stuff of international politics; the questions, apparently moral or ideological as much as political, which determine the contours of international postures.

It is in the Third World that most of the crises of the last twenty years – Cuba, the Middle East, Vietnam –

1. Quoted in *International Herald Tribune*, 14 November 1973. (Author's italics.)

have occurred. They were born in the social and political consequences of colonialism and bred in the atmosphere of the cold war. Colonialism conditioned the underdeveloped world to a state of dependence; attempts to break that state generally resulted in the substitution of one metropolis for another and absorption into the global confrontation. With the changes in world politics, new attempts are being made, and new metropolises are emerging.

According to the classic colonial pattern, under-developed countries produced one or two commodities – either minerals, such as copper, ore, or diamonds or cash crops, such as cotton or tea – for export to the colonial metropolis. The revenue from these exports was spent on imported luxuries for the local oligarchy, invested abroad or repatriated as profits from foreign-owned mines or plantations. During the twentieth century, this pattern has changed mostly on the surface.

A number of countries have embarked on a pro-gramme of industrialization either from necessity because economic links with the metropolises were broken during the depression and the Second World War or as a positive part of the universal attempt to raise living standards. Some have nationalized mines or plantations and even carried out mild land reforms to distribute land and wealth more fairly and create incentives for improved efficiency. But these measures have tended to incorporate such countries even more tightly into the world economy. Industrialization has merely substituted the import of essential machines and semi-manufactured products for previously inessential luxuries. The cost of these imports, often combined with worsening terms of trade, has led to an ever-spiralling syndrome of indebtedness. As well as repatriated profits, the revenue from exports returns to the metropolis in the form of debt repayments. Economic growth, attendant upon industrialization, has barely sur-passed the increase in population and in some countries standards of living have actually fallen. Nationalization and land reform have rarely done more than transfer privileges from one elite group to another. Only a few states with valuable primary commodities such as oil have escaped this depressing story.

At the same time, these developments have increased awareness of the problems. Industrialization and population growth have created new urban classes, frustrated by their situation and ready to embrace nationalist or socialist philosophies offering hope for change. Where the international situation has allowed such groups to achieve and hold on to power, as in Egypt or India, they have sought some measure of independence by turning to new sources for aid, credit or arms and to new markets. During the 1960s, when the US had more influence over Western foreign policies, they turned to the Soviet Union; now, Europe and Japan may be the preferred alternatives. In the process, however, their local and particular problems have tended to become part of the world power struggle and their territories a focal point for confrontation.

This kind of development is most pronounced in the Middle East. The area has always been caught in the political struggles of great powers and it is there that the shifting nature of great power alignments first becomes apparent. Just as the end of European colonialism was signalled in the Suez crisis of 1956, so the new Atlantic rivalry and the fading of East–West confrontation emerged in the oil crisis of 1973.

Arab nationalism took root during the Second World War. A number of countries – Egypt, Syria, Lebanon, and Iraq – were cut off from foreign supplies and forced to develop local industries to cater for the domestic market and the Allied troops. Ideas which had been mooted among the intelligentsia and the soldiers for a generation at least spread to workers, professionals, local entrepreneurs and even peasants. They embraced widely varying shades of opinion, being influenced both by socialism and by fascism,[1] but they shared one consistent line of thought – a commitment to Arab unity and to the defeat of imperialism.

1. There were 'iron shirts' in Syria and 'green shirts' in Egypt.

Arab nationalists came to power, after the war, in Egypt, Syria, and later Iraq, through the intervention of the armed forces. They turned to the Soviet Union to obtain weapons because the alternative was membership in a Western military alliance,[1] which was viewed as equivalent to American hegemony.

The relationship with the Soviet Union reflected all the contradictory elements of global relationships. It was made possible by the relative independence of these regimes, situated as they were at the interstices of the declining European empires and emergent American power, and it strengthened their radical tendencies. And yet, paradoxically, the Soviet desire to avoid confrontation ultimately limited the possibilities for independent action. Soviet aid and Soviet arms enabled these countries, particularly Egypt, to pursue radical policies at home – nationalization of foreign enterprises, build-up of heavy industry, elimination of feudal landowners, social reform, etc. – and a militant policy abroad. Aid to the oil industry, for example, made nationalization possible. There were some strains in the relationship, as when Communist parties were banned or when Iraq suppressed the Soviet-supported Kurds, but dissatisfaction did not really make itself felt until the Six Day war of 1967.

During that war, the Soviet Union failed to come to the assistance of the Arabs until after the fighting was over. When US and Soviet clients actually met face to face, it became abundantly clear that the Soviet desire to avoid confrontation was greater than its support for the Arab cause. The humiliating defeat of the Soviet-equipped Arab armies could not have been more harmful to Soviet prestige in the area.

The war lost Egypt £100 million or more in

1. In the early 1950s, the Western powers attempted to consolidate their hold over the Middle East by creating a Middle East Defence Command. They withheld the supply of arms 'except for the purposes of internal security and regional defence'. Iraq, for example, joined the Baghdad Pact, in 1955, because this was the only way she could acquire Western arms.

annual foreign exchange earnings – £80 million in Suez Canal revenues and £20 million in profits from the Sinai oil-fields. There was also a big drop in the receipts from tourism. In consequence, Egypt, whose cotton crop was, in any case, mortgaged to the Soviet Union for years ahead, was more than ever dependent on Soviet aid. The new relationship was brought home to the Arabs by the influx of Soviet advisers and technicians (in part, of course, to fulfil the badly needed training requirements of the Egyptian armed forces), by the granting of Egyptian air and naval facilities to the Soviet Union, and by the Soviet refusal to supply, to any of the Arab countries, offensive military equipment. With the increases in oil revenues accruing to Egypt's Arab allies, Egypt was able to purchase European arms and technology. But it was not until after the Yom Kippur war and the Sinai disengagement, when the US promised aid worth billions of dollars and such things as nuclear reactors, that Egypt was able to dispense with the Soviet presence. In 1975, Egypt abrogated the Treaty of Friendship and Cooperation and withdrew facilities for Soviet warships. Since then, Egypt has been negotiating with Britain and France for aid in establishing an independent military industry.

Other Arab nationalist states have also sought to diversify their suppliers. Syria has also signed agreements with the United States, Europe, and, in one instance China, while Iraq and Algeria are buying arms from France. And while these states are moving towards Europe from the Soviet Union, the oil-rich Arab states are approaching from another direction, namely the United States.

The rapid growth of the oil industry, during the 1960s, brought major changes in the traditional monarchies of the Middle East. Around it, there developed a new middle class which, as in Egypt and Syria before, formed the nucleus of an Arab nationalist movement. In Libya, Arab nationalists overthrew the monarchy in 1969; elsewhere, kings and sheikhs retained their positions through responding to domestic demands. The world was surprised in the crisis of 1973 by the forthright position adopted by the formerly conservative King Faisal of Saudi Arabia, and by the fact that the most hostile postures towards Israel were taken by Kuwait and Libya. Yet perhaps because the nationalists in these countries owed their livelihood to oil or perhaps because of the wealth bestowed by oil, their stance was in many ways less radical than in Egypt, Syria and Iraq. They wanted a greater share of the income from oil, but they were not prepared to dispense with the West altogether. They feared the spread of left-wing guerrilla groups such as those in Dhofar or Yemen. They were deeply religious and bitterly opposed to communism. Their opposition to the United States was less ideological than practical. They objected to America's support for Israel and they objected to the dominance of American oil companies. Only by breaking this dominance, by playing the major oil companies against the independents in Europe and Japan, could they secure increased participation in the oil industry and increased revenue. Prince Abdullah Abdul Aziz, now Prime Minister of Saudi Arabia, has expressed the line of the oil monarchies. In a speech in January 1974 he said:

> If the winds of US policy continue to fill the sails of Israel, as they do today, the momentum of history may join ourselves and the Europeans in a unique and deep friendship.
>
> The European states are working for a United States of Europe, which means that they will eventually become completely emancipated from the influence of world giants.
>
> Europe's emancipation will destroy the monopoly control of the major powers over international politics and give the Arabs the means of power which hitherto have been the exclusive preserve of the Soviet and American giants.

And, in a more practical vein, he added that there 'exists a high degree of reciprocity between our interests and theirs. For our part we need European expertise in the field of land reclamation, industrialization and armaments. The

Europeans need our oil, our other raw materials and our markets.'[1]

The Europeans welcome the new 'reciprocity'. Not just because they get independent access to oil, but because new vistas open for industrial markets, in general, and order-starved defence companies, in particular. Long before the energy crisis, France was prospecting the Arab market and had organized deals with Saudi Arabia, Kuwait, Libya and Iraq, ranging from oil pipelines to desalination plants or the construction of telephone exchanges; not to mention the important orders from Arab countries for Mirage aircraft and other French weapons.[2] Since the Yom Kippur war, all the European countries, as well as Japan, have come forward with greedy offers of industrial goods for oil. Even Germany is beginning to find that the lucrative Arab prospects can overcome war-time guilt. For some time, the Community has been formulating a 'single overall policy' for the Mediterranean and, now, the first steps have been taken in establishing an EEC–Arab 'dialogue'.[3] Despite popular support for Israel, the traditionally pro-Arab Foreign Offices of Britain and France are in their element. While the Arabs may regard Europe as a radical alternative to America and Russia, Europe regards the new relationship as a continuation of historical ties that were temporarily interrupted. Britain forgets the Balfour Declaration, the Sykes–Picot agreement[4] and the war-time riots against her, remembering only the romance of Lawrence and their joint battle against the Turks. France regards the relationship with Israel (mourned only by the aerospace

---

1. *Guardian*, 9 January 1974.

2. Between 1967 and 1972, French exports to the Arab world, excluding the Mahgreb – Algeria, Morocco and Tunisia – where France has always had important interests rose fourfold, making France the largest exporter of industrial equipment to the Arab world.

3. After American protest, the Europeans have agreed to exclude political questions from their discussions.

4. The Anlgo-French agreement in 1916, to divide up the Arab world between them, in violation of pledges given by Britain to the Arabs.

industry) as a calculated aberration lasting only so long as the Algerian war. As for the Italians, the Mediterranean policy was their idea, back in the 1950s when Mattei of ENI punctured the international oil cartel.[1]

But in forging the new Arab relationship, the Europeans will have to face America; this is why the first round of the Euro-American game was played on the battlefields of the Middle East. The Yom Kippur war and the ensuing oil crisis brought forth an unaccustomed statement of independent foreign policy on the part of the European Community – and this was true of Japan as well. It also exacerbated disputes with America about the role of NATO and of oil.

The most important American clients are the two most powerful countries in the region – Israel and Iran. Israel has no alternative to America; she is isolated by world opinion. But Iran is playing big power politics. In addition to huge purchases of American arms, bringing thousands of American military advisers into the country, Iran has also signed industrial, technical and military agreements with Western Europe and the Soviet Union. The Shah, who regained power in 1953 with American backing in a *coup* which suppressed Iran's own nationalist movement, gained his freedom to manoeuvre from the détente with the Soviet Union and the growing independence of Europe. But as new lines of international confrontation are drawn up, Iran may be caught up in a new position.

Already, hostility is developing between Iran and its Arab neighbours. Iran's defence budget is the largest in the area, now amounting to $6 billion a year, and its armed forces are equipped with some of the most sophisticated aircraft, missiles, tanks, and naval vessels in the world. The Shah has made it clear, on many occasions, that his aim is to make Iran defensible against any enemy in a non-nuclear war, and that it is necessary to build up a

1. There are, of course, divisions in Europe on this question – the Dutch and the Danes tending to favour Israel. But in the event of European union, it can be assumed that they will follow the French and British lead.

defence capability to match *all* potential trouble-makers in the area combined:

> We have to develop such a potential to keep the area secure after the British leave. Iran can do it because we have no territorial or colonial designs. Iran's role in the Persian Gulf is to present the image of strength, wisdom, and absolutely altruistic purposes and, yet, without any thought of trying to play Big Daddy.[1]

But Iran's intentions have already been belied by the seizure of three islands in the Persian Gulf, Abu Musa and the Greater and Lesser Tumbs, on the departure of the British in 1971. Long before that, however, relations with Arab countries were becoming strained. Iran had a long-standing series of disputes with Iraq, over navigation in the Shatt-al-Arab, offshore oil rights, the Kurds, and Iranian access to Shiite holy places in Iraq. A border dispute erupted in early 1974. Also, the main Iranian oil-fields are situated in Khuzistan, an area inhabited by Arabs with a nationalist bent. Their movement for independence has received support from Iraq and Egypt. Before 1967, when there was a war in the Yemen, Iran developed ties with the Arab monarchies. Now they too share Arab nationalist suspicions about Iranian intentions in the Gulf and about the various forms of military and industrial cooperation that Iran has developed with Israel. There is also talk of a growing confrontation with another sub-imperialist power, India.

It may be that potential conflicts are suppressed by renewed American internationalism. The United States has also, since the Yom Kippur war, developed closer ties with Arab nations, particularly Saudi Arabia. A reassertion of American influence over European foreign policies might limit the alternative suppliers for radical nationalist regimes to the Soviet Union or China, providing a renewed expression of apparent East–West conflict.

The alternative, the prospect of a new Middle Eastern confrontation, Arabs versus Iran and Israel, sup-

1. Quoted in SIPRI, *The Arms Trade with the Third World*, Penguin Books, 1975, pp. 222–3.

ported by Europe and America respectively, is still a matter for speculation. So is the idea, often voiced in what the Chinese call 'second world' circles, that the new 'sub-imperialist' powers, the oil-rich Arab states, should challenge the super-power *status quo*, the Arab–Israeli peace established by the United States with tacit Soviet concurrence, with the help of the Europeans. But the fact that the speculation is made, and is often treated as prediction, is part of a dialectical process in which the integration of Europe could provide the wherewithal for an alternative Arab stance, and a growing polarization in the Middle East could represent an impetus towards European independence.

Outside the Middle East, potential occasions for Atlantic conflict are apparently remote. Yet one that is little known and little talked about might be found in Latin America. In 1967, a Peruvian decision to purchase Mirage aircraft from France provoked a suspension of US economic and military assistance. The supersonic fighter had become a symbol of Latin American independence, since the US had expressed determination to keep such planes out of the region. And the Peruvian action marked the beginning of a Latin American movement away from the United States. Nearly ten years later, the Peruvian purchase of Soviet MiG aircraft received little public notice.

Latin America has had its own version of nationalist discontent, a version that is often suppressed by the blanketing hold of the United States. From the mid 1960s, however, with the rising cost of aid and foreign wars and the emergence of Atlantic rivalry, nationalist movements found that domestic American constraints on the exercise of power in the Southern hemisphere and the accompanying new-found readiness of European countries to challenge that power gave them a certain freedom to manoeuvre. In the mid 1970s, a series of *coups* and international financial restraints proved the limits to such freedom. These were associated with the reassertion of American international authority. Should the US revert to a parochial position and Euro-American competition re-emerge, it is possible to conceive of a Latin America transformed from a US back-water, whose revolutions sometimes make the second page of European newspapers, to a forum for Euro-American struggle, whose revulsions are anxiously watched by the world.

Nationalism in Latin America has much in common with Arab nationalism. It was said of APRA (American Popular Revolutionary Alliance) in Peru that 'it combines anti-American nationalism, a certain Marxist influence, involvement with the Indian past, definite elements of fascism, and even an application to history of Einstein's theory of relativity.'[1] Similar statements could perhaps be made of Peronism in Argentina, Getulism[2] in Brazil, Acción Democrática in Venezuela or MNR (National Revolutionary Movement) in Bolivia. They are less concerned than their Middle Eastern counterparts with the question of unity, and they face more competition – and sometimes cooperation from peasant and worker movements on the revolutionary left. What they all share is opposition to US imperialism.

Industrialization is generally much more advanced in Latin America than in the Middle East. Latin American countries achieved their independence in the early part of the nineteenth century, and the depressions of the 1880s and the 1930s and the Second World War gave nationalist movements the opportunity to embark on a programme of industrial autonomy.[3] The Second World War, however, also gave the United States the opportunity to consolidate

1. Marcel Niedergang, *The Twenty Latin Americas 2*, Penguin Books, 1971, p. 114.

2. After Getulio Vargas, President of Brazil, with short interruptions, from 1930 to 1954.

3. Attitudes to such movements have not really changed since the nineteenth century. *The Times* of 28 April 1891 wrote of President Balmaceda of Chile, overthrown by pro-British conservatives backed by English money, in the same year: 'There is in Chile, a communist government, a despot or various despots who under the false name of Executive Power have overturned all the peace, all the prosperity of the preceding eighty years.' Quoted in André Gunder Frank, *Capitalism and Underdevelopment in Latin America*, Penguin Books, 1971, p. 118.

its hegemony over the area and to eliminate all traces of the European influence, which had been so important during the previous century. After the war, nationalist governments, where they existed, were overthrown by military *coups*, directly or indirectly supported by America, or severely constrained by their forced dependence on American markets, credit, arms and technology.

Nationalist parties retained their popularity, if not their power, and the strength of the opposition was brought home in the stoning of Nixon, then Vice-President, on a tour of Latin America in 1958. The dangers inherent in the situation – the dangers that produced Cuba – led to a new initiative, the Alliance for Progress, promulgated by Kennedy as the great liberal alternative to underdevelopment. Yet the most that the Alliance for Progress achieved was an increase in the profitability of US companies operating in the area. In 1968, Mr Covey Oliver, the joint US Secretary for Inter-American Affairs, revealed that Washington's financial aid to Latin America was 'relatively modest in relation to the return'.[1] It was during this period that a number of revolutionary movements made their appearance, following the example of Cuba.

But in the mid 1960s, the situation began to change. Governments began to seek non-military solutions to internal insurgency. Military regimes in countries like Argentina, Peru and Bolivia began to adopt elements of nationalist programmes, enunciated by the revolutionaries they opposed and civilian regimes in countries like Colombia found they could make timid steps in the direction of independence without provoking an irate American response. This was made possible in part by increased Congressional scrutiny, following the high-handedness displayed in the Bay of Pigs and the Dominican Republic episodes, but, more importantly, it was made possible by

1. Quoted in Marcel Niedergang, *The Twenty Latin Americas 1*, Penguin Books, 1971, p. 11. According to one estimate, net capital inflows to Central America in the period 1960–71 rose by 344 per cent, while net capital outflows increased by 982 per cent. (Bert Rosenthal quoted in Barnet and Müller, op. cit.)

the increased willingness of Europeans to penetrate an American preserve.

France was, naturally, the first to respond to Latin American requests for arms. The American response to the Peruvian aircraft purchase did not deter Argentina, Brazil, Colombia and Venezuela from concluding similar deals. Britain was, initially, more susceptible to American pressure, but, observing the advantages reaped by France, she joined Germany in participating in the Latin American naval build-up, initiated in the late 1960s. This build-up was, at least in part, directed against US fishing vessels who refuse to recognize the 200-mile limits now being claimed by several Latin American countries.

The arms deals opened the way for economic penetration. An Argentine deal for French armoured cars was associated with the establishment of a Renault assembly plant, while the sale of naval frigates to Brazil allowed for increased British participation in the Brazilian steel industry. More generally, however, a number of countries have begun to recognize that by seeking ties with Europe, they can improve the conditions of dependence, make, so to speak, a better deal with the imperialists. A joint communiqué, issued by President Frei of Chile and President Lanusse of Argentina in 1970, stated that it 'seemed indispensable to seek concrete formulas which would permit the propounding of *new and more equitable bases* for commercial relations, finance, transport and technology to the countries of Europe'.[1]

This kind of thinking was largely confined to Spanish America, however. Since 1964, when Goulart – a successor to Vargas – was overthrown, Brazil has been governed by a particularly brutal and reactionary military regime. Its very conservatism has attracted US multinationals, who have enabled the Brazilian oligarchy to reap the benefits of a phenomenal rate of growth, while extracting an ever larger surplus from the over-exploited peasantry. European and Japanese companies have also benefited from

1. *Latin America*, 16 January 1970. (Author's italics.

this development, but this did not, initially, undermine the Brazilian position as America's most favoured and lucrative ally. (More recently, however, a Brazilian–German deal for nuclear reactors has provoked American disapproval.)

The move to Europe on the part of Spanish American countries was in part directed against the growing economic pull of Brazil. At his inaugural celebrations, President Lleras Restrepo of Colombia established the foundations of the Bogotá Club which later became the Andean Group, comprising Colombia, Ecuador, Peru, Bolivia, and Chile. In 1973 they were joined by Venezuela. Unlike the Latin American Free Trade Area (LAFTA), made moribund by the rivalry between Argentina and Brazil, and by the participation of foreign businessmen, the Andean Group members shared a common interest in restricting the power of Brazil and the influence of foreign capital. In addition to agreements on the freeing of trade and the pooling of merchant fleets, their most celebrated decision required foreign companies operating in the area 'to transfer 51 per cent of their share to local investors over a period of 15 years in the cases of Colombia, Chile and Peru and over 20 years in the cases of Bolivia and Ecuador', and prohibited such companies from repatriating dividends of 'more than 14 per cent of invested capital, except in special cases, where the commission [of the Andean Group] might waive this condition'.[1] (Since the *coup*, however, Chile has ignored this stipulation.)

Judged in an Asian or Middle Eastern perspective, these restrictions are not, perhaps, very radical. But then the members of the Andean Group are not attempting to insulate their development from the world economy. Only socialist Chile attempted that and, in the process, was destroyed. The alternative path of Cuba, towards the Soviet Union, may no longer be open to Latin American countries now that détente takes precedence. Rather, the regimes in the Andean countries are concerned to build a more independent and profitable relationship with the advanced

1. *Keesings Contemporary Archives*, 13–20 November 1971.

industrialized nations. The leading exponent of this tendency is Peru. The Peruvian Minister for Economic Affairs
explained at a meeting of the Inter-American Development
Bank that neither communism nor capitalism can assure
economic independence for Latin America:

> Communism, which destroys the essential free-
> doms of a democratic regime, and capitalism, which
> admits them in a restricted form provided they submit to
> its interests and unilateral pressures, are not acceptable
> patterns of development for the national majorities of
> an underdeveloped people.[1]

In pursuit of its independent policy, Peru signed a cultural,
scientific, and technical cooperation treaty with France,
and a number of commercial agreements with Eastern
Europe and with China. Peru also opened its border to
Japan; trade with Japan has increased rapidly and Japanese
companies have been involved in metal working, automobiles, shipbuilding, food processing, mining and petro-
chemicals.[2]

Closest in political outlook to Peru was Peronist
Argentina. Argentina was attracted to the Andean Group
by her long-standing rivalry with Brazil. This rivalry,
which makes itself felt in a number of specific disputes
about the river Parana or about Antarctica,[3] concerns
fundamentally the competition between the two industrial
poles of Latin America. The Argentine military regime,
which came into power in 1966, embarked on a 'Plan
Europa' for building up Argentina's defence industry with
European help. Later the 'Plan Europa' was extended to the
civilian sphere, and the economic plan, announced in 1970,

1. *Keesings Contemporary Archives*, 6–13 November 1971.
2. There have always been close ties between Japan and
Peru: there are sizeable Japanese communities in Peru and children's
story books, in Japan, suggest that the Incas are of Japanese origin.
3. The river Parana runs through Argentina, Paraguay and
Brazil. Paraguay, traditionally an Argentine satellite, has recently com-
plied with a Brazilian decision to exploit the river for hydroelectric
power. Also, a Brazilian scientific expedition to Antarctica, an
Argentine preserve, has annoyed the Argentine government.

provided for large amounts of finance, capital goods, and technical know-how to be sought from Europe and Japan. The new regime's policy was carried to its logical conclusion when, in 1973, it agreed to the return of Perón, the nationalist hero of the late 1940s and the early 1950s.

During his exile in Spain, Perón had been laying the basis for a European–Latin American 'Grand Design'. He sought out the European chauvinists, mending his fences with the Catholic hierarchy in Rome (the church had helped to bring him down in 1955), and establishing close relations with such leading industrialists as Marcel Dassault and Agnelli of Fiat. The plan envisaged that 'Italy [there has been a strong Italian influence in Argentina due, in part, to the presence of sizeable Italian communities] should spearhead a combined European penetration of Argentina, which will provide a counterpoint to North American and Japanese investments.' Europeans and Latin Americans will halt the advance of powerful multinational corporations through

> a new breed of international company, with the participation of public sectors, as well as of private sector capital, from both sides of the Atlantic; but United States and Japanese capital would be excluded. The Europeans would have the smaller share of the equity – between 30 and 40 per cent – in these new corporations, but would benefit from the new relationship.[1]

On achieving power, Perón established close links with Peru, and to a lesser extent, Cuba, the Andean Group, and Mexico – which, despite its geographical and financial proximity to the United States, has been diversifying its economic relations towards Europe and its neighbours and also began to build up a relationship with Arab countries.

Argentine hopes of a Spanish-speaking alliance were severely damaged by the *coup* in Chile, in which, as has now become public knowledge, the US government and American economic interests were deeply implicated.

1. *Latin America*, 6 April 1973.

Then came Perón's death and more recently the right-wing military *coup* which overthrew his wife and successor. Furthermore, the *coups* in Bolivia (1971) and Uruguay (1973) brought these two countries within the Brazilian sphere of influence. Both in Chile and Argentina, international financial pressure played a critical role. (In Argentina, a badly needed IMF loan was announced two days after the *coup*.) In Peru, financial conditions imposed by the international banking community have been explicitly linked to the abandonment of some of Peru's more radical domestic policies. The pro-American backlash in these countries is the less well known underside of American policy towards Latin America which is accompanied by a new public offensive, strikingly reminiscent of the approach to Europe. Kissinger has talked of a new 'partnership', in which Latin Americans must be treated as equals, and has said that 'we can not afford to let our political relations and our economic cooperation be distorted by commercial quarrels.'[1]

It should not be concluded, however, that Latin American nationalism has been decisively defeated. All this is merely the reflection of America's renewed assertion of international authority. As the US economy comes under strain and as European integration proceeds, such things as the unity of financial interests will come apart and new opportunities for radicalism will appear. As in the Middle East, the one reinforces the other and as the West veers from Atlantic rivalry to East–West confrontation, so Latin America is likely to veer from independence and international conflict to loyal obedience and domestic violence.

Africa is different because there the Europeans are less the challengers than the challenged. The European relationship with black Africa is much more firmly entrenched than its relationship with the Latin Americans or even with the Arabs. Unlike the Middle East, the European imperial role was never really interrupted there. The United States had, in the past, little interest in penetrating Africa – except of course the Southern part – and the Soviet

1. *Washington Post*, 18 April 1974.

Union had little opportunity. Nationalism has been much more subdued than in the Middle East. Industrialization has been very limited, and the urban classes, like their counterparts in the oil-rich Arab nations, are dependent upon the international relationship. While they may support an increased return from that relationship, they are not concerned to change it fundamentally. In the early 1960s, the intellectual heroes of the liberation movements, like Nkrumah of Ghana, embraced a more radical philosophy, calling for Pan Africanism and opposition to imperialism and several of them turned briefly to the Soviet Union and China. But they lacked mass support and were rapidly snuffed out by Western-backed military *coups*, with the notable exceptions, of course, of Tanzania and Zambia and their new allies in Southern Africa. It was said that the OAU, which is all that remains of Pan Africanism, was 'transformed from a radical force seemingly capable of offering real resistance to the further subordination of Africa to Western capitalism, into a conservative alliance guaranteeing the stability of existing neo-colonialist structures'.[1] The liberation of the Portuguese colonies and the revolution in Ethiopia may represent a new transformation.

The OAU is the forum through which the African countries are defining their relationship with Europe. Under the Yaounde Convention, which expired at the end of 1974, the former French and Belgian colonies in Africa were given associate status in the European Community. This allowed for free or preferential trade between the African countries and the Community, for aid from the European Development Fund and the European Investment Bank – some $1 billion between 1971 and 1975, and for a set of common institutions. With Britain's entry into the Community, a similar form of association was negotiated for the African, Caribbean and Pacific Commonwealth members, together with Ethiopia, Sudan and Libya under the Lomé Convention. This covers all of black Africa, except Liberia (virtually an American colony). The

1. Giovanni Arrighi and John S. Saul, *Essays on the Political Economy of Africa*, Monthly Review Press, New York, 1973, p. 86.

Arab North African countries – Tunisia, Morocco and Algeria – who have negotiated separate agreements, attended the EC–OAU talks as observers. The new relationship has been welcomed on both sides, particularly among the francophone nations, as a continuation of the old, and has been praised in fulsome chauvinistic terms. According to President Leopold Senghor of Senegal:

> [Euro-Africa] is an idea which I came across in 1935 . . . when reading the German philosopher and ethnologist, Leo Frobenius, who maintains that, until the neolithic age, there had not been two separate civilizations, one European and the other African, but a single civilization. The arrival in Europe of the Indo-Europeans brought about bipolarization and at the same time a complementarity, a symbiosis, which led to the development of the first and most brilliant civilizations in history, those of the Mediterranean. Through the Euro-African association, we today can build a new civilization which will be the driving force behind the civilization of the twenty-first century which Teilhard de Chardin called La Civilisation de l'universel.[1]

The universal civilization won't for the time being include South Africa. However conservative the OAU may have become, it is held together by its ideological opposition to colonialism and to the white regimes of Southern Africa. An important question, therefore, is how or whether the Euro-African association will draw Europe into a confrontation with the South.

Europe has an enormous stake in Southern Africa. Britain, alone, has more than £1,000 million invested in South Africa, and a further £200 million in Rhodesia. South Africa is Britain's biggest earner of investment income overseas. US investment has also increased rapidly in recent years, but it has not yet overtaken Britain's.

The continued profits from these investments depend on South Africa's continued growth and this, in turn, depends on the expansion of South Africa's market.

1. Interview with Europa, *The Times*, 4 December 1973.

There is little room for internal expansion, for this might erode apartheid – the basis of the South African government. Nor can South Africa as yet compete in the advanced industrialized markets of Europe, North America and Japan. The alternative is black Africa, and South Africa has been pursuing the potential of northward expansion through its policy of 'dialogue'. 'Dialogue' also has a political function; friendship with black Africa would neutralize the external support for the black opposition within South Africa. This policy received a considerable setback with the independence of Mozambique and Angola and the extension of the guerrilla war in Rhodesia. Yet, for Europe, its success would have been a great blessing; it would enable her to maintain the special relationship without risking, indeed rather enhancing, her stake in South Africa.

      This situation poses a dilemma for American foreign policy. On the one hand the United States could support the European position in Africa ostensibly to prevent Soviet penetration in order to hold the West together. This would involve support for the South African government, with concessions such as majority rule in Rhodesia and independence in Namibia to obtain support from conservative black African governments, and the isolation of socialist regimes such as those in Mozambique and Angola and the dubbing of revolutionary groups as 'pro-Soviet' or communist – in other words, the creation of an African anti-communist ethos which would blur the racial conflict and justify Western solidarity. On the other hand, the United States could oppose the development of Euro-Africa by offering an alternative to European hegemony, by abandoning the white regime in South Africa as domestic black pressure groups would urge, and neutralizing the more radical nationalist regimes.

      Both courses of action are evident in the ambivalence of recent American policy towards Africa. The 'internationalist' anti-communist approach was apparent in the American opposition to the dominant guerrilla group in Angola, MPLA, even before the Cuban intervention

Zaire and, perhaps, in the recent negotiations in Southern Africa. But in Kissinger's emphasis on Africa for the Africans, his publicity stated opposition to hegemony and to blocs in Africa, it is reasonable to suppose that he was referring to the vestiges of European imperialism as well as to the Soviet Union, an attitude which could well become more prominent should parochialism come to the fore again.

The rapid political changes in Africa and the evolution of new alliances and confrontations are, like the developments in the Middle East and Latin America and, in different guises and different importance in other places, an essential part of the changing relationships between advanced industrial nations. New domestic needs and political struggles in rich countries are not insulated from trends in the Third World or from events, like the Yom Kippur war, in which the various elements of the international system are focused in a crisis. The growing importance of the Third World may draw Europe and America into support for rival political factions and, indeed, for rival nations like Saudi Arabia versus Iran or Argentina and Peru versus Brazil. As European nations move closer together and become more powerful, local political rivalry could develop into ominous forms of confrontation, and provide some of the political reasons or even excuses for Atlantic conflict. Alternatively, such rivalry might be suppressed and traditional patterns of Third World politics re-established with renewed emphasis on Soviet aggression as the justification for renewed suppression of nationalist movements. But this would depend on the suppression of certain developments in the Atlantic region which prompt new initiatives in the Third World and are moulded by new rivalries there. It would depend on domestic crises in the advanced industrial nations, particularly in Europe and individual European nations and how they are surmounted.

9   Europe

Europe, according to Altiero Spinelli, has entered a
'moment of creative tension':[1] a moment when the forces
for both integration and disintegration are building up,
when a resolution one way or another seems imminent. On
one side are the fast-growing corporations chafing against
the barriers to their expansion, represented by the nation
states. On the other are the people in the slow-growing
regions of Europe who would suffer from that expansion.
Caught in between are national governments, whose survival depends on corporate expansion and whose demise,
nevertheless, would result from integration.

The moment is characterized by a series of apparent
victories and defeats for the European cause, by momentous
decisions, which are rapidly overtaken by events. The
European movement has never been more active; its
solidarity was greatly enhanced by America's decline; the
withdrawal from Vietnam, the domestic crises, and the fall
of the dollar. The Community is enlarged, and has affirmed

1. Altiero Spinelli, *The European Adventure*, Charles Knight
& Co. Ltd., London, 1972, p. 15.

its identity and the Commission puts out an unceasing flow of proposals for integrating, coordinating, and above all 'harmonizing' every kind of industrial, foreign, commercial, scientific, fiscal, technological and competitive policy that can be imagined. Every so often, the Europeanists are filled with exultation as their leaders proclaim once again their commitment to achieving economic and monetary and even political union. And equally often, they are plunged into despair by exchange rate changes, protesting farmers and housewives, border taxes and subsidies and even import controls, which threaten to bring the whole painstakingly built European edifice down in ruins.

The logic of the present situation, based on the analysis developed earlier,[1] would indicate a limited number of outcomes. One, based on the dictates of continued corporate expansion, is the dissolution of the European nation state – the creation of a European union and the unfolding of Atlantic conflict. Another is the retention of the present political system, under renewed American tutelage, with stagnation, domestic violence and repression and a renewal of the ideological confrontation between East and West. The third, which is much less predictable, would involve radical changes in social structure, abandoning the fundamental principles of private enterprise, in at least some European states. All these outcomes are hard to imagine; we have coped with compromise for so many years. What follows is an attempt to explain why and how the compromise is breaking down, domestically and internationally – it is an attempt to translate the logic into plausible political developments.

The 'moment of creative tension' began with the dollar crisis. But it was based on the contradictions which had developed from the partial integration of the European Community. As we have seen, the formation of the European Community was based on an alliance between fast-growing European corporations and the governments of fast-growing regions based in Lotharingia,[2] who wanted to

1. See Chapters 1 and 3.
2. See Chapter 1.

dismantle national economic barriers to further expansion, and, on the other hand, national producers and peripheral nation states, who wanted a wider and more powerful protection for the smaller nation state. The abolition of internal tariffs and the commitment to full currency convertibility, seen as a first step towards a liberal world economy, satisfied the former; while the Common External Tariff, the Common Agricultural Policy, and the preferential relationships involving special trade agreements and development aid established with former colonies initially satisfied the latter. Since then, three additional nations have joined the Community and a regional policy, which provides some limited compensation to peripheral regions, has also been established. There has also been a certain amount of collaboration on 'high' technology projects, although this has not formally taken place within the Community framework.

It was inevitable that the liberalizing aspects of the European Community should exacerbate the tendency for uneven development, that corporations should concentrate their production in the fast-growing areas of Europe, where the greatest profits could be made and where the foundation for further expansion could be laid. This unevenness was reflected in trade imbalances. The fast-growing areas not only experienced rapid increases in exports but their increased income was spent as much on goods produced at home as on goods produced abroad. Hence West Germany and the Netherlands, for example, experienced growing trade surpluses as well as full employment and rapid economic growth.

This was not the case for the peripheral regions of Europe. Although France and Italy, measured as a whole, experienced relatively fast rates of growth in the 1960s, this was concentrated in a few large-scale enterprises, both nationalized and private, which have adopted modern processes and techniques and which are confined to particular regions – in France, Paris and the north-east, and, in Italy, the north. Elsewhere, in west and south-east France and southern Italy, the economy remains predominantly agricultural while large, but diminishing, numbers of small and medium-scale enterprises continue to exist. The propensity of these sectors to import as the economy expands is greater than the propensity of the advanced sectors to export; or to put it another way, the expansion of the large advanced corporations accompanying the abolition of tariffs was not sufficient to offset the decline of the older and more backward sectors when subjected to foreign competition.

Take Italy, for example. When Italy joined the EEC, her main competitive advantage lay in the abundance of labour. During the 1950s, profits and productivity rose much faster than wages with the result that when the internal European tariffs were lowered, Italy found herself able to flood the European market with light engineering goods and petro-chemical products, which she could produce much more cheaply than elsewhere. Indeed, during the first decade of the Common Market, Italy was able to establish herself, within the EEC, as the greatest exporter of clothing, shoes, domestic electrical appliances, petroleum products, cement, artificial and synthetic fibres, textiles other than cotton, and canned food.

But these advantages could only be maintained at great social cost. During the 1950s, industrialists were able to keep wages down because of the existence of widespread unemployment, amounting to around 10 per cent of the labour force and massive migration from the south.[1] But by the early 1960s, much of this reserve labour had been used up and workers were in a stronger position to demand and obtain increased wages. Although this did not erode the competitiveness of established Italian exports, it resulted in domestic inflation and a rapid increase in imports, particularly beef, for which the growth of exports could not compensate. The result was a trade deficit, the flight of capital abroad, and the imposition of deflationary measures which brought an end to the economic 'miracle'.

The Italian economy recovered and expanded

1. Between 1959 and 1963, 1·6 million people left agriculture to find jobs in industry.

during the mid 1960s, but it never again achieved the heady miracle-era growth rate of 8 per cent or 9 per cent. Moreover, industry only recovered sufficiently to finance its own continued expansion in the north. It did not provide the wherewithal to solve the drastic problems of urban overcrowding, inadequate housing, and the continued poverty of the south. Such increases in income as there were during the period totally obscured the social dislocation and suffering caused, at both ends, by migration. In 1968 the students began to revolt and, in 1969, they were joined by workers. The 'hot autumn' of 1969 and the subsequent protests resulted in substantially improved conditions for workers. It also led to a rapid increase in imports, a slowdown in exports, stagnation in income, continued domestic unrest and a flight of capital abroad.

The peripheral regions of Europe were multiplied when the Community was expanded in 1973. In particular, an unwilling recipient of the effects of uneven development is Britain, whose economy was not so much backward and agricultural (as in the underdeveloped regions of France and Italy) as old, or, to use a politer economists' expression, 'mature'. This 'maturity' is reflected in the predominance of declining industries – shipbuilding, coal and steel, the decay of early industrial regions, the small proportion of labour employed in agriculture (4 per cent compared with 15 per cent in France and 8 per cent in Germany) and hence the drying up of the industrial labour supply, and the degree of concentration in British industry.

In other words, Britain had long since reached the point, which is now being approached by the United States, in which the relationship between investment and innovation in the dominant sectors breaks down and in which slow growth, balance of payments deficits and overseas investment sets in. By 1970, British overseas investment accounted for 20 per cent of the world total and, today, a large part of that investment is going to Europe.

The effects of entry into the European Community on Britain, Denmark and Ireland were drowned in the dollar crisis and the rise in oil prices which greatly increased the disparity between regions and sectors. The devaluation of the lira, franc and pound and the revaluation of Lotharingian currencies against both the dollar and each other resulted in a faster rate of inflation in the peripheral regions than in Lotharingia. Furthermore, the increase in the supply of international money used to finance the trade deficits caused by the increase in oil prices resulted in a transfer of resources from the periphery to the centre. Increased oil revenue was spent more on goods produced in Lotharingia than on goods produced in the declining regions of Britain, Italy and France (and also Denmark and Ireland), while growing speculative balances were increasingly entrusted to the safest currencies, notably the German mark and the Dutch guilder. Nor did the exchange rate changes result in competitive advantages for the peripheral regions. This was largely because of the multi-nationalization of the economies of these regions. Already in 1969, for example, one third of British trade consisted of transfers between subsidiaries of the same firm, while the sales of overseas subsidiaries were several times larger than exports. Quite apart from the fact that big multinational corporations are not likely, in the short run, to increase the competition with their overseas subsidiaries or to dislocate international production processes, the various price-fixing arrangements to which they are subject makes them unwilling to lower export prices in response to devaluation and hence expand exports. Furthermore, the rapid inflation, resulting from the rise in oil and food prices as well as devaluation, eroded the competitive advantages that smaller, price-conscious, home-based firms might have expected to obtain. Indeed, in so far as governments took deflationary measures, e.g. cuts in public expenditure, wage restraint and increases in taxation, to reduce expenditure on imports and free resources for export, this also paradoxically stimulated inflation since large multinational corporations tend to raise prices when demand falls in order to maintain a steady income.[1] The result was the now familiar

1. This argument is put forward at greater length in Chapter 3.

combination of inflation, unemployment, stagnation, and balance of payments deficit in the peripheral nations of Europe. In so far as some governments were able to solve balance of payments, problems, this was at the cost of increased unemployment.[1] Indeed, in Britain and Italy, real income actually fell.

It was not merely that the liberalizing aspect of the European Community exacerbated the problems of the weaker nation states and indeed that the various measures such as so-called non-tariff barriers taken by these states threatened to jeopardize the whole basis of European integration, by destroying the customs union. It was also that the protectionist elements of the Community, notably the Common Agricultural Policy, failed to come up to expectations. This policy, as we have seen, was based on the principle of charging the same high prices throughout the Community, so as to assure the farmer of an income which compared favourably with what he might earn in industry. It was threatened, in part, by exchange rate changes which led either to drastic changes in price and hence trade diversion – for example, a revaluation of the mark against the EEC's unit of account, based on gold, would involve a fall in prices to the consternation of German farmers while a devaluation of the franc involved an equivalent rise in food prices to the consternation of the French consumers and industry – or, alternatively, to the imposition of border taxes and subsidies, as in fact occurred in Germany and Benelux, and was quite contrary to the famous European 'spirit'.

The policy was also threatened by its own weakness. The prices were determined on the basis of long and arduous political bargaining by the governments involved. The result was that they satisfied no one, except possibly large French cereal producers. They were too high to assure an adequate diet for the lower income groups in

1. The growth of the British oil industry may solve the balance of payments problem but little else; additional income is likely to be used to reinforce the existing industrial structure, while public expenditure is increasingly restrained by inflation and ideology.

Europe, who, for example, were forced to shift their consumption from butter and meat to margarine and cereals. And they were too low to assure an adequate income to farmers in Germany, Benelux and the mountain areas of Italy and France. Farmers have expressed their protests graphically by herding cows into ministerial meetings at Brussels. In addition, the relative levels of prices encouraged an imbalance in agricultural production; high wheat and dairy prices encouraged the production of cereals and milk products, of which there was already a surplus, while the production of meat, of which there is an acute shortage, was discouraged.

The absurdity of the agricultural policy has reached its apex in the ever-growing butter mountain. The price for butter is so high that the farmer produces much more than the consumer can afford to eat. The agricultural fund buys the excess butter which, in 1972, amounted to 15 per cent of the total European butter consumption. Community officials are faced with the choice of letting it melt or go bad, feeding it to pigs or selling it to the Russians. In 1973, they adopted the latter alternative and half the butter mountain was sold to the Soviet Union at the cut price offer of 8p a pound. (British consumers then paid 25p a pound and European consumers paid around 70p.) The Soviet Union resold the butter to Chile at a profit, adding greatly to the Community's embarrassment.

The same solution for the Community 'wine lake' was vetoed by the British. The production of cheap Italian wine brought the price of French wine down to guaranteed CAP prices and resulted in protests from French wine producers, the imposition of a French ban on the import of Italian wine, and a wine lake of 2,400 million litres. Instead of selling the wine to Russia, the Community have adopted a more expensive proposal to distil 460 million litres into industrial alcohol.

Finally, of course, the price policy is a substitute for other policies, involving subsidies to poorer farmers, redistribution of land in certain areas, modernization and structural improvements. The 'orientation' section of the agricultural fund has money available for such purposes but it has been quite inadequate. It is evidence of the astounding failure of the policy that the President of Confagricoltura, the association which primarily comprises those large Italian landowners who could be most expected to benefit from it, should have come out with a strong condemnation in October 1969:

> In agriculture we tried to speed up the process of integration: reaching the single market, reaching the common prices, without tackling what ought, to our way of thinking, to have been the primary policy to follow, that is, without tackling the policy of the real and genuine structure of agriculture. Common prices were dreamed up for agricultural products; it was imagined that a common agricultural market could exist, independent of advances, independent of progress in all other sectors. It was a great mistake.[1]

The mistake has got to be rectified but the fear is that in doing so the European cause will take a step backwards. The agricultural policy is practically the sole testament to European integration now that the dollar crisis and oil prices have caused such havoc with the customs union. And although, in the words of one eminent European Commissioner, 'no one who is not French or a first generation European could shed a tear to see it go.'[2] there might be many tears should it mark the fizzling out of Europeanism.

It is this situation which has increased the urgency of further progress towards a European Union. On 9 February 1971, the Council of the European Community passed a resolution expressing the Ministers' 'political will to introduce, in the course of the next ten years, an economic and monetary union'. The union, based on the so-called Werner Plan, is expected to comprise the establishment of a single currency and of a European central bank, and the 'harmonization' of national budgets, i.e. equal rates

1. Quoted in F. Roy Willis, *Italy Chooses Europe*, Oxford University Press, New York, 1971, p. 148

2. Anonymous article, attributed to Dr Ralf Dahrendorf, in *Die Zeit*, quoted in *The Times*, 2 August 1971.

and types of taxation and social spending. The first stage of the plan was completed on 31 December 1973. It involved the joint float of European currencies, except sterling and lira, against the dollar, the reduction of fluctuations in internal exchange margins to $2\frac{1}{4}$ per cent, some limited measures of tax harmonization such as the introduction of VAT, and the establishment of a European Monetary Cooperation Fund in Luxembourg. Its fragility, however, was exposed by the floating of the French franc in January 1974. The second stage, which was intended to run from 1974–6, will establish fixed exchange rates, bring Britain, Ireland, Italy and presumably France into the float, introduce closer 'coordination' of economic policies, free capital movements, and enhance the powers and the budget of the cooperation fund. About the third stage, both governments and commission are notably vague. Indeed, it is clear from the failure to complete the second stage, the opposition of the current British government, and from the mumness on the subject, that, for the time being, the union is in abeyance.

The important point, as all concerned must know, is that the plan for economic and monetary union, in the absence of political union, is untenable. As it stands, it will work rather like the gold standard in the nineteenth century was supposed to work: trade adjustments are brought about automatically through deflation and unemployment in the deficit regions. Of course, this is what happens now within a single country; a trade deficit between Vermont and New York, for example, or Wales and England, makes itself felt by unemployment and falling income in Vermont and Wales, and by labour migration to New York and England. But there are important differences. One is that the integration of the federal American budget or the British national budget involves a built-in redistributive mechanism, however inadequate. By paying taxes to the central government on the basis of income, and getting back social benefits on the basis, at any rate in theory, of equality; the slow-growing regions receive more from the central government than they pay in taxes. Under the Werner Plan, the regions will have to finance their own expenditure out of their own taxation (although they will get some regional aid), increasing rather than decreasing the deflationary burden. If, despite the redistribution entailed by fiscal integration, Vermont and Wales remain depressed, as we know they do, then it is unthinkable to impose the degree of suffering that might result from monetary integration, in the absence of such safeguards. Moreover, unlike the proposed Werner Plan, Wales and Vermont have not got independent governments through which their protests can be expressed – failure of the Vermont State government to solve Vermont's economic problems can be blamed on the Federal Administration. It is inconceivable that a European national government could stand by and watch the flight of jobs and income to some other part of Europe. Either it would be overthrown through the electoral process or it would have to take emergency measures, involving increased repression and, quite probably, violence. In other words, the unspoken assumption that underlies the vagueness about stage three is that economic and monetary union must involve political union. There will have to be a Community budget, based on direct taxation rather than the revenue from customs duties and government subsidies, and that budget will have to come under the control of a European government. Further, in order to overcome the political difficulties faced by national governments, the European government will have to represent the ultimate European power – it will have to be able to overrule national governments – and presumably, given the European commitment to parliamentary democracy, it will have to be based on direct election. Finally, the European power will have to be backed by force; otherwise national governments might be tempted to secede. (There is also the minor difficulty of 'harmonizing' defence budgets.) In other words, political union would mean military integration as well.

On the face of it, the climate for political union is not altogether unfavourable. President Giscard d'Estaing has called for a new initiative, arguing that 'the modern world will only really be modern when the map no longer shows in the place of Europe a torn hole' and that there can be 'no alibi for those who have been summoned to a rendezvous with history, as is the case with our generation, and who leave empty-handed'.[1] This appeal has resulted in the establishment of regular summit meetings, known as the 'European Council', a secretariat for political cooperation attached to the Council of Ministers, and the decision to introduce direct elections to the European Parliament in 1978. Since most political parties and groupings nowadays take support for European union for granted, additional moves towards political union might be expected. Indeed, part of the British Labour party and the French Communist party stand out as pointed exceptions and even their opposition is based on the form rather than the principle. But the reality is considerably more complex.

European political parties are formed on the basis of class and religion. The classic right–left distinction divides the Conservative and Liberal parties, based on business and landed property and committed to the free enterprise system with varying degrees of emphasis on state intervention and social reform, and the Socialist parties, based on industrial and agricultural workers. The rudderless professional middle classes veer between the two, generally towards the former, and can often tip the political balance. Superimposed on this structure are the religious parties. These are generally much looser political groupings which cover a much wider social spectrum. They tend, however, to be dominated by the upper end of the spectrum and, in Benelux, Germany,[2] and Italy, the Catholic parties, under various names, play the role of conservative parties elsewhere. From time to time, as in Germany and France immediately after the war and periodically in Italy, there are left-wing outbursts from the Catholic trade unions. Finally, there are other local and particular divisions that make

1. Broadcast of August 1974, quoted in *Keesings Contemporary Archives*, 24 February–2 March 1975.
2. In Germany, the Christian Democrats include Protestants. Although the leadership is careful to strike a balance between Protestants and Catholics, it remains, in effect, a Catholic party.

themselves felt in the political structure; such is the linguistic division in Belgium between Flemings and Walloons and such is the division over the treaty with Britain between the two main Irish parties, Fine Gael and Fianna Fail, both Conservative and Catholic.

In general, the Catholic parties have been passionate supports of the European cause. Indeed, it can be said to be the one issue which unites them. In the early post-war period, this derived from the Vatican's unalterable opposition to socialism.[1] This merged with the development of a European chauvinism and the idea of Europe as the resurrection of the Holy Roman Empire. Successive Popes put their wholehearted support behind the European movement, particularly in the 1950s when the prospect of a Christian Democratic European government, following, at any rate implicitly, the directions of the Vatican, seemed perfectly plausible. Another, and perhaps more important, political reason for their Europeanism was the fact that, except in Germany, Christian Democrats always found themselves at the head of highly unstable governing coalitions. Precisely because they were such loose and all-embracing parties, they could rule only through alliances of one faction or another with other political parties. These difficult alliances had to be maintained, in order to prevent, at any rate in the 1950s, a radical left alternative. Europe represented a way out of this political dilemma. When it came to the crunch and this, above all, lay beneath their Europeanism, they were the parties of business and the supporters of the *status quo*, even if the *status quo* meant a change in the geography, if not the essence, of the social system. Today the Catholic parties retain their governing role only in Italy and Benelux.

Of the declared supporters of the *status quo*, the conservative parties, only the extreme right, the British

1. This opposition is not shared throughout the Catholic hierarchy. The worker priest movement in France was suppressed in August 1953 by Pope Pius XII, who talked of the 'alarming spread of revolutionary ideas' among the priesthood, but has revived since 1966. In Italy Catholics and Communists have, in recent years, emphasized the similarities in the teaching of Christ and communism.

Powellites, the orthodox Gaullists, and the neo-Nazis in Germany, retained their commitment to the nation state by the early 1970s. The more moderate conservatives – currently governing only in France – support the idea of European union, but temper their support in the Gaullist and Churchillian tradition, with talk of confederation and the 'independence and personality' of the nation state. At the same time, they tend to be the harbingers of imperial visions; Pompidou illustrated the conservative position in his request to the National Assembly 'to join your efforts with mine as witness to our faith in the greatness of France within a Europe that is mistress of her own destiny'.[1] In the near future, the conservative parties could slow down the progress to political union by insisting that they retain the appearance of national sovereignty.

Further to the left are a mass of smaller parties, variously called liberal, republican or radical, which have their roots in nineteenth-century liberalism. Many of these parties were powerful strongholds of business in earlier times when business was the revolutionary rather than conservative class and that basis is not forgotten. Further, ideological liberals are also federalists; the Italian Republican party, for example, is the party of Mazzini, one of the greatest of the nineteenth-century federalists. None of these parties, however, has achieved power in the post-war period, except as a relatively unimportant coalition partner.

In the years to come, the crucial political determinant will not so much be the Catholic and right-wing parties, for in the end they will probably follow the dictates of corporate expansion, but the attitudes and strategy of the parties of the working people. All these parties, in Europe, have their roots in the nineteenth-century socialism based, fundamentally, on Marxist tenets. But the great divide lies between the Communist and left Socialist parties, who have remained more or less faithful to those

1. Pompidou, message to the National Assembly and Senate, 5 April 1972, quoted in *Keesings Contemporary Archives*, 20–27 May 1972.

tenets, and the Social Democrat parties, whose ideology is strongly tinged with nineteenth-century liberalism. This liberalism is expressed in the commitment to parliamentary democracy which has caused the Social Democrat parties to veer from left to right and back again according to the intensity of social conflict, and the exigencies of power. Whereas the Communist parties can, if they choose, maintain a consistent set of political principles and wait for the popularity that comes with crisis, the Social Democrats, with an eye on the next election, must adapt their stance to the prevailing mood. The prolonged economic 'miracle' of the 1950s and early 1960s brought major changes in the outlook of Social Democrat parties. At a time when workers were experiencing rapid increases in their standards of living they found it less necessary to register their cross on ballot papers and, in any case, were less concerned about achieving change. To improve their electoral position, therefore, the Social Democrat parties turned increasingly to the professional middle classes, the famous 'floating' voters, and moderated their philosophy accordingly. The British Labour party turned to Butskellism (a term which referred to the pinkish Conservative, Butler, and the purplish Labour leader, Gaitskell) but the protests from the the left prevented it from renouncing its theoretical commitment to public ownership and popular management. The German Social Democrat party went a stage further and, at the Bad Godesberg Convention of 1959, it adopted 'an outspokenly revisionist programme, which proclaimed the party's attachment to Christianity, the profit motive, and a programme of moderate social reform'.[1] These adaptations were successful in so far as they enabled Social Democrats to enter government, in some form or other, in every European country, except France and Ireland,[2] during the 1960s.

1. *European Political Parties*, P.E.P., George Allen & Unwin Ltd, London 1969, p. 35.
2. The Irish working class is extremely small. The Labour party has never achieved more than 16 per cent of the vote since it lost its Northern industrial base and remains permanently in opposition.

It was not merely that political moderation won more votes, but that Social Democrat leaders themselves, and indeed the unions with which they were linked, were infected by post-war economic expansion. There was a general sense that the Keynesian revolution had brought an end to capitalist crises and that capitalism, harnessed to economic growth and social reform, was a relatively humane system. Some went so far as to argue that the replacement of owners by salaried managers would, ultimately, transform class differences. This view was even extended to sectors of the Communist party. In an article in the Italian Communist journal, *Rinascita*, shortly before his death, Palmiro Togliatti, the Communist party leader, speculated that 'the classical class struggle no longer made sense in Western Europe'.[1]

Along with these developments went a more enthusiastic attitude towards Europe. In the early post-war years, Social Democrats were ambivalent. On the one hand, many Social Democrats were as rabidly anti-communist as their conservative opponents – the experience of communist infiltration tactics, of the Stalinist line in the Spanish Civil War and, above all, of the 1939 Hitler–Stalin pact had left a bitter legacy. In addition, the liberal anti-war element in their philosophy attracted them greatly to federalism, and many Social Democrats led the way in creating a Europe-wide – both East and West – federal movement. On the other hand, many socialists recognized the 'brutal realities' of Europe, 'in its institutional form, hidden behind its federalist, progressive, idealist mask'.[2] Pietro Nenni, the leader of the Italian Socialist party, described the proposed European Political Community as a 'colossal "cartel" intended to guarantee permanence of profits to capital and stability to the governments'.[3]

But as the Social Democrat parties began to moder-

1. Quoted in Norman Kogan, *A Political History of Post-War Italy*, Pall Mall, 1966, p. 189.
2. Lelio Basso, left-wing Italian Socialist leader, quoted in Willis, op. cit., p. 303.
3. Quoted in Willis, op. cit., p. 304.

ate their opposition to capitalism, so they also looked with
greater favour on the creatures of capitalism, notably the
European Community. Because the Common Market was
associated, in time, with the economic miracle, they drew
the conclusion that the Common Market helped to explain
the miracle as much as vice versa. Or, to paraphrase a well-
known aphorism, because what was good for the big
corporations in the 1950s and 1960s had proved good for
the economy as a whole, they believed this would continue
to be the case in the 1970s and 1980s. In addition, of course,
the Common Market was a fact. And, what is more,
within the European Community as a whole, the Social
Democrats were the single largest political grouping. Unlike the early 1950s when the Europe of the Six was
Christian Democrat, in the 1970s, a Europe of the Nine
would undoubtedly prove to be Social Democrat. While for
some, this potential was registered in a merely opportunist
fashion – for the right wing of the British Labour party,
perhaps – for others, it was sincerely believed that, by
joining forces, Social Democrats could humanize the
European Community. So it was that the Social Democrat
parties, with the exception of the British and Irish Labour
parties, were in the forefront of demands for direct elections to the European Parliament and for such reforms
as improved regional and social policies and greater control
over monopolistic practices.

Their lead was followed in a much modified form
by the European Communist parties. The Soviet invasion
of Czechoslavakia in 1968 and Brezhnev's subsequent
assertion that the Soviet Union had the right to intervene
in a socialist country to prevent the restoration of capitalism
was the occasion for European Communist parties to
declare their independence from Moscow.[1] Their new
independent stance had involved a commitment to parliamentary democracy and, like the Social Democrat parties,
a new appeal to middle-class voters. 'The taking of the

1. Already in 1956, after Khruschev's denunciation of
Stalin, Togliatti had said that the Soviet model was no longer obliga-
tory for other parties and advocated a 'polycentric' system.

Winter Palace, the long march, the Commune of 1871 or the barricades of Berlin in 1879 – that is all history,' according to a French party theoretician, 'The working class of modern France is no longer the proletariat that Marx described, nor that of Lenin.'[1] In particular, the Italian Communist party has, for some time, favoured a policy of accommodation with the Christian Democrats.[2] The strategy of the party has always been based on the Gramscian notion of inserting the party into a political position that could upset the traditional hold of the ruling classes over the spread of ideas and culture, and progressively shift the social and political situation.[3] In pursuing this strategy, the party has emphasized its administrative efficiency and has campaigned on the slogan 'Participation in Italian political life'. The lead of the Italian party has been followed, more or less, by most other European Communist parties, except that in Portugal. The French Communist party has developed a joint but somewhat strained electoral strategy with the socialists.

In keeping with this change of stance, the Italian Communist party relaxed its opposition to the European Community as early as 1963, while the French party has

1. Quoted in *International Herald Tribune*, 28 September 1976.
2. Recently, theoreticians have emphasized the similarities in the teachings of Marx and Christ. A joint statement by the French and Italian parties in November 1975 affirmed full support for co-operation between Communists and Catholics: 'Today, large sections of Catholics are becoming increasingly conscious of the contradictions between the realities of imperialism and capitalism and their profound aspirations towards human brotherhood, social justice, the affirmation of higher moral values and the full expansion of the human personality.' (*Keesings Contemporary Archives*, 30 April 1976.)
3. Bruno Trentin, a member of the Communist Central Committee, and a leader of CGIL, the Communist trade union, defined the CGIL policy as 'a policy of *presence*. The CGIL does not try to prevent the modernization of Italian capitalism. Instead of opposing neo-capitalist solutions *a priori*, we each time oppose more advanced and equally realistic and concrete solutions to them. There is nothing opportunist about this; by moving with a dynamic situation, our revolutionary demands only gain greater relief . . .' Quoted by Perry Anderson in *New Left Review*, nos. 13–14, January–April 1962.

adopted a policy of moderate support for Community Institutions in its joint programme with the Socialists. In part, support for the European Community can be seen as an element in a new international policy, which involves opposition to all military blocs, to US imperialism[1] and, implicitly, to Soviet hegemony in the European Communist movement. It also entails the renewal of relations with China and support for the Chinese idea of Europe as part of the 'second world' or the 'intermediate zone' between the super powers and the underdeveloped world. But equally, support for the European Community was the logical consequence of the policy of presence and reform. For the French left alliance, the aim of participation in the European Community is 'liberating the domination of capital, democratizing its institutions, supporting the workers' claims and orientating community achievements towards their interests'.[2] Similarly, Giorgio Amendola, a reformist member of the Italian Communist party, has said that Italian Communists want to build a European Community 'because multinational companies can only be fought with multinational powers, and these powers can be efficacious only if they have a democratic basis by means of elections by universal suffrage to the European Parliament'.[3]

Thus it appears that only a few small left-wing Socialist parties in Denmark, Italy and France, together with parts of the British Labour party, seriously oppose

1. The left in Italy was perhaps the European grouping most conscious of the reality of American hegemony. The Allied occupation, when partisan bands were disarmed and debarred from power and when popular factory councils were dismantled and former managers tainted by the Fascist regime restored and the American threats issued before the 1948 and 1952 elections and at the time of the formation of NATO were sufficient to convince Italians that the possibility of a left-wing government coming to power, while Italy remained within the American orbit, was very remote. As Europe moved towards an independent position, so it became conceivable that within Europe lay the possibility of achieving power.

2. Statement of the Union de La Gauche Socialiste et Démocrate, quoted in *Keesings Contemporary Archives*, 22–29 July 1972.

3. Quoted in *Keesings Contemporary Archives*, 30 April 1976.

further steps towards European integration and it might be thought that the obstacles to political union are few. But this assumes that the present political alignments will be maintained and that policy can be translated into practice. Sheer bureaucratic inertia and political haggling over the form that union will take – the Gaullists and Conservatives supporting the sovereignty of the Council of Ministers for example and the Social Democrats supporting the sovereignty of Parliament – will slow down the process of integration and, in so doing, stresses and strains will appear which could make or break the union.

In Germany and Benelux, the pro-European solidarity is likely to be maintained. Any measure of integration can only speed up their ever-growing economies. Germany and the Netherlands have experienced steady expansion since the end of the war. Furthermore the advent of Social Democrat governments in Germany, in 1969, and in Holland, in 1973, has smoothed the path to European union by bringing their foreign policies more in line with the rest of Europe. In particular, Willy Brandt's Ostpolitik weakened, in appearance at least, the Atlanticist commitment and made possible a more independent European foreign policy and closer cooperation with France. Belgium has also been a beneficiary of the Common Market and is likely to continue to be so. The establishment of the Community, with its headquarters in Brussels, enabled Belgium, with the encouragement of hefty tax concessions, to attract large amounts of foreign capital. From being a declining iron-, coal- and steel-based region, Belgium was able to join the Lotharingian club.

The crises which will make or break a European union will not take place in Lotharingia but in Britain, France and Italy.[1] It is in these countries that the negative consequences of European union are to be experienced and that the compromise which currently holds the European Community together is breaking down. In all three countries, there have been important changes in the political

1. Denmark and Ireland are likely to follow the lead of their largest customer – Britain.

spectrum in recent times. The sucking of resources from declining and underdeveloped regions has provoked the rise of regional protest movements. In France, a number of autonomist movements, often adopting violent methods of struggle, have arisen in Brittany, the Basque provinces, Occitania (Languedoc) and Corsica; while in Britain, Scottish and Welsh Nationalists have built up substantial electoral strength, reflected in a significant parliamentary presence – and this is not to mention the civil war in Northern Ireland. The squeezing of small businessmen and peasants – what the French call the 'independents' – has resulted in Poujadist tendencies within the British Liberal party, the French Gaullists, and the Danish People's party as well as the development of extreme rightist parties. Finally, and most importantly, the stagnation, and even in some instances decline of real wages, the growing un-employment, the narrowing gap between manual and intellectual workers and the pressure to increase the inten-sity of work has stimulated the left-wing parties and rein-forced their new ideas and images.

In Italy, the policy of accommodation with Catho-lics has given rise to the idea of an 'historic compromise' between the Communist party and the Christian Demo-crats, in which the Communist party would join a coalition government with the Christian Democrats. As the largest party in Italy, the Christian Democrats have dominated every one of the numerous, ineffective unstable and short-lived coalitions that have theoretically ruled Italy since the war. Because of the substantial electoral gains made by the Communists in recent years, the 'historic compromise' or a popular front with the Socialists is likely to become a reality within a few years. The present Italian government survives on Communist sufferance and the Communists now control six parliamentary commissions. In France, the left alliance is also gaining strength despite failure in the 1978 elections and, in Britain, the left of the Labour party has greatly increased its influence over the party, if not the government.

All three left groupings have remarkably similar

programmes. They are all committed to a struggle with multinational corporations, to the control of international movements of capital and goods and to the democratization of all levels of society, especially the organization of the work place. Yet commitments such as these represent and are seen to represent a threat to the continuing basis of capitalist society and could only be carried out against the bitter opposition of important sectors of the middle class, both national and multinational, as well as the state itself. As two Italian Marxists have put it; to achieve the stable alliance between big business and the working class, which is presupposed in the 'historic compromise', it would

> be necessary to alter the *nature* of production (services in place of individual consumer goods) as well as its *market* (giving priority to the domestic market over the foreign one on which capitalist development has been based, especially during the boom of the fifties and sixties). It would be necessary radically to reorganize agriculture, in order to ease the terrible food shortage. It would be necessary to impose Draconian cuts in the current spending of the state bureaucracy, that enormous siphon of waste and parasitism created by the Christian-Democratic Party in its own image and likeness: in other words, it would be necessary to strike at broad sectors of the middle class.[1]

And one might add the international community, since all these measures would be deeply opposed by the United States as well as the other members of the EC. Indeed, it is possible to anticipate, at least in France and Italy, violence possibly involving military intervention as well as dangerous rifts within the security forces, should these programmes be carried out.[2]

1. Paolo Flores and Franco Moretti, 'Paradoxes of the Italian Crisis', *New Left Review*, no. 96, March–April 1976. (Italics in the original.)
2. There is considerable unrest within the French and Italian armies, particularly among badly paid conscripts. These are

The alternative, however, is to remain within the rules of modern multinational capitalism and to take measures to solve the economic difficulties which are bound to provoke further protest. These measures include drastic cuts on all public spending except defence, i.e. reduction in spending on education, health, social services, housing, etc., increased taxation, and wage restraint. This is, essentially, the course adopted by the British Labour government, in opposition to majority views of the party and at the cost of electoral support. It can be maintained only so long as the government enjoys the collaboration of the unions, the left-wing members of Parliament and the Liberal party. As grass roots protest mounts, the government may have to submit to electoral defeat or a party split. The long-term success of a strategy of this kind is equally improbable, for similar reasons, for a left alliance government in France or for a government in Italy in which the Communists participate.

In other words, the compromise between the multinational corporation, on the one hand, and national producers and workers, on the other, that has served the peripheral nation state in the past is breaking down and the conflict, reflected in the changing pattern of politics and the failure of traditional economic policies, is becoming very difficult to manage within the framework of the democratic nation state. What are the possible outcomes?

One is the radical transformation of society, as envisaged in the programmes of the left-wing parties. This may not be a plausible outcome. Even if the left-wing parties were allowed to achieve power, the effective use of power is fraught with international pressure, domestic conflict, and popular antagonism, that could only be resolved through a long and unpredictable struggle that could

supported by French army officers – many of whom are said to have voted for the Socialist leader, François Mitterand in the Presidential election of 1973 – who resent the poor conditions, bad pay and under-equipment of the French army, resulting from the expense of the *force de frappe*. In Italy, it has recently been revealed that *coups* have already been attempted by right-wing generals with covert American backing.

perhaps only succeed through combined action in all three countries.

The second, which is the multinational solution and perhaps the necessary condition for continued Lotharingian expansion, is the dissolution of the nation state, a European union in which domestic unrest would appear relatively minor and localized and in which, it might be hoped, fragmented peripheral protest movements would gradually wither away. This is the kind of solution that might be expected should moderate Conservatives or Centre coalition governments, perhaps even with Socialist participation, along the lines of the present British Labour government, succeed in holding on to power and evading more extreme domestic conflict for a sufficiently long period of time. This is the more plausible, the more parochial is American foreign policy; American withdrawal would give greater scope for broad-based political alliance, as in Italy, for example, and, simultaneously, allow the development, as occurred in the late 1960s and early 1970s, of an anti-American Europeanist ideology which is widely shared by different political strands.

Finally, there is the stalemate solution, reminiscent perhaps of the Bonapartist *coup*. This is the solution in which the nation state is strengthened and a right-wing government carries out the only measures possible within the rules of multinational capitalism, through repression instead of popular consent, with recurrent and worsening economic crises and increasing indebtedness to the United States or to international institutions dominated by the United States. Theodore Geiger, a distinguished authority on Atlantic questions, has recently concluded that

> some if not all of the existing European governments could be compelled by the magnitude of their economic difficulties and the prospect of losing elections to popular front coalitions to appeal for American help . . . In the longer term, the centrist democratic governments or dictatorships replacing left-wing regimes would be likely to lose popular support, at the same time that they

would be confronted with economic recovery problems beyond the capacity of their individual nations to solve. They too would have to turn to the United States.[1]

This solution is perhaps the inevitable consequence of the failure of the other two possible outcomes. It would involve the build-up of the army and police, the externalization of domestic conflict in the ideology of the cold war, and the justification for military build-up in renewed emphasis on the Soviet threat. In a sense, it is not a solution, merely the prolongation of crisis.

1. Theodore Geiger, 'A New US Hegemony in Western Europe?', National Planning Association, March 1974.

10   Future Prospects

Thinking about the future needn't be prediction. Prediction is dangerous because there are too many things to be taken into account. If one could physically take everything into account, then one would create a mental mirror of reality – something one would comprehend as little and as slowly as life itself. Instead, one must generalize; one must abstract those things that seem important in the present and consider how they might develop. The problem is that the things that will seem important in the future may be hardly detectable now and even if some brilliant intuition suggests a new phenomenon which might emerge, there is so little experience and so few words with which to understand it.

Thinking about the future ought to be an exercise of imagination rather than an extrapolation of past trends. One has to emphasize some things at the expense of others, to decide what things will become more significant and what things might disappear. But this judgement is inevitably based on an analysis of the present which is, of its nature, partial and predisposed towards the assumptions of the past. The very language in which it is expressed is the language of history. And so predictions, which cannot escape traditional categories of thought, are, of necessity, qualified by 'ifs' and 'buts' and 'assuming thats'. What follows is an attempt to describe the alternative possibilities that arise from the analysis in this book. Because they depend on certain assumptions about the continued functioning of the present social systems, they cannot be called predictions and they cannot be considered exclusive – they might not come about.

The key to the argument and the basis for antici-pation is the tendency for uneven development, the ten-dency for some regions, industrial sectors, social classes and even individual corporations to become wealthy at the expense of others. This tendency follows from one im-portant assumption about the nature of Western society; namely, that its basis is corporate expansion arising out of a competitive system of private enterprise. This assumption is not necessarily inviolable or inevitable. Indeed, it is challenged at a number of different levels and the challenge is a direct consequence of the economic and social trends we have described. This is not the place to embark on a description of the possible ways in which the fundamental assumption of society might be overturned or of what might come afterwards; that would be the subject of another book. But a few preliminary remarks should perhaps be made.

The most powerful challenge to Western society comes from socialist and autonomist political groups in Italy, France and, to a lesser extent, Britain. As we have seen, these groups are based on the increasing casualties of the social system. Workers in slow-growing sectors may lose their jobs or suffer declining standards of living. Com-munities in slow-growing regions may also witness the migration of people, the break-up of families, the deterior-ation of public amenities, the appearance of the tourist or weekend resident. Alternatively, expansion of a kind may proceed artificially, in a way that is degrading to workers and consumers through the tedious production of items that benefit no one – arms, waste paper, bits and pieces added to existing products.

The ability of such groups to achieve and hold on to power might perhaps be discounted, such is the conservatism of the institutions of society – the armed forces, the civil service, the church, etc. – and such is the strength of international pressure. But it can be argued that the very same crisis that produced the changing constellation of political forces is reproduced within the state as a whole and, beyond, in the world at large. Bureaucrats must surely become conscious of the irrationality of their position. Obedience to the principle of corporate expansion yields domestic economic decline and social conflict and, in so doing, undermines the legitimacy and financial basis of the state itself. It is not simply an irrationality of economic policy, for it runs through every aspect of social activity. Take the military sector, for example. The purchase of elaborate and expensive weapon systems, like battle tanks and aircraft carriers, is part of the ideology of a new European war, tactically much like the last one, in which the Soviet Union plays the part of Nazi Germany. It is around weapons such as these that NATO is organized and held together; they could perhaps be described as the symbols of the solidarity of the Western world. Yet European governments in declining regions cannot afford these weapons; they save on other things like support equipment and pay. And the weapons themselves are hardly appropriate to the real battle conditions of modern times. Soldiers, situated in Northern Ireland, the North Sea or the Basque provinces (as a result of economic decline and social conflict), where they may be ill-prepared, over-equipped and underpaid, must surely find the ideology of Soviet aggression somewhat remote.[1]

Nor is it just through the strains of administration that the opportunity for new social movements could arise. There is also the ambiguity of international relations.

1. It is irrationalities of this kind which explain the public protest of French conscripts and the widespread support for the French Socialist leader Mitterand among French army officers.

Earlier, we tried to describe the deepening American dilemma as Atlantic rivalry emerges and international corporate expansion increasingly comes into conflict with domestic American goals. America can continue to act as an international authority, relying more and more on the instruments of repression and ideology as the domestic economy weakens. Or it can pursue parochial interests, and abandon the West to economic warfare and political confrontation. This dilemma has its counterpart in Lotharingian indecision, that is to say the indecision of the German, Dutch or other stable European governments about whether to treat left-wing movements as a threat to international corporate expansion, or as potential partners in the European enterprise. It is in this shifting world preoccupation between East–West and Atlantic confrontation that apparently isolated local social change could seem plausible. And this, of course, would raise a whole new set of issues – alternative social formations, new barriers to international corporate expansion, new forms of social disintegration within Lotharingia and America and a new set of possible scenarios – a North–South confrontation in Europe, a socialist Europe, new splits in the communist world – all, for the present, within the realm of speculation.

Without such changes on a fairly widespread scale, the prospects for the future are sombre. If the European centre parties succeed in creating a European union, then one can anticipate a degenerating Atlantic conflict. We have argued that capitalism needs a single world authority in order to guarantee the liberal conditions for international corporate expansion. Once American power is challenged by a state backed with similar wealth or military strength, the idea that international institutions can undertake these functions with a minimum of friction seems somewhat Utopian. A European government will have the power, real or perceived, to resist American demands for trade concessions, for a dollar or dollar-backed SDR-based monetary system, or for continued privileges for US oil companies. But it won't have the power to impose its own demands – stable exchange rates and deflationary policies for deficit countries or low international fuel prices. It will be able to back clients in the Third World, to penetrate or maintain politically protected markets or access to raw materials. But it won't be able to establish secure spheres of influence; it will always face competition from America. In other words, one can anticipate the transformation of current apparently rhetorical squabbles into real economic disputes and, thence, into crises in the Third World, like the Yom Kippur war, which provide an accumulation of mistrust and even hostility – the basis for political conflict.

Even if the logic of the argument is accepted, that real material interests are involved as well as the stability of society and state, and even if the facts are accepted, Germany's current status as an economic super power and Europe's future status as a political super power, this quarrel between West Europeans and Americans may still seem fanciful to those grounded in the friendship of NATO and the Marshall Plan. But this is to misunderstand the nature of a European Union – something which is altogether different from the sum total of nine unstable European States. A future European government will be moulded as much by its immediate political environment as by European tradition. And that environment will encompass the various crises – about oil and dollars and food and conflicts in the Third World – through which Atlantic conflict will evolve. In its very creation, in other words, a European government will be anti-American.

Nor is it just through external events that Atlantic sympathy can be expected to erode. For a future European government is likely to be authoritarian and militaristic. It will be authoritarian because of the stresses and strains of unity. Peripheral protests won't disappear because a European government is established. On the contrary, it is only the power to make such objections felt that will be muffled. In a Europe as a whole, peripheral peoples will be disaffected minorities, instead of the majorities they might represent within a smaller nation state. They will be kept in order through a combination of repression and paternalistic 'development' programmes. The fact that these same minorities – the British or the southern Italians – are those with closest cultural and family ties to powerful communities within the United States cannot but antagonize American leaders. American sympathy for British rebels against a European government, for example, could be likened to American sympathy for Irish rebels within the United Kingdom.

A European government is likely to be militaristic because of the important role played by the defence industry and the Community bureaucracy in its formation. One of the most important pressures for a European union stems from the need to rationalize European arms companies and create a common defence policy. Likewise, the existence of a European administration – already overblown – is, at once, a permanent lobby and a probable basis for a European Union. In addition, a future European government is likely to be dominated by West Germany and this means that, in terms of tradition, it is more likely to be a government of Bismarck than of Gladstone. It would not be exaggerated to suppose that to Americans, this combination of paternalism, state intervention and repression may well be seen as little more than a moderate variant of fascism – or communism.

These perceptions, moreover, need not be one-sided. There has always been an important strand of anti-Americanism in European public opinion – one which stems in part from American hegemony in Europe and is expressed in terms of the distaste for the American failure to deal with problems of poverty and racism, the American support for reactionary regimes abroad, the corruption of administration, and the neglect of public services. None of these aspects of American behaviour are likely to diminish; on the contrary, the evidence and the argument suggests that domestic economic problems will exacerbate them. If one also takes into account the differing international images likely to be presented by Europe and America – European support for Latin American and Arab nationalists, together with black Africa, increased trade and other exchanges between Europe and the socialist countries, American support for Brazil, Israel, Iran and even perhaps South Africa – one has the kernel of an ideological conflict.

Nor is it entirely far-fetched to suppose that the combination of economic conflict, political disagreement and ideological confrontation could entail war. Nobody would dispute the potential for small-scale wars in remote parts of the world in which European-equipped troops fight American-equipped troops – after all, this happens already. And it would not be thought extreme to envisage the direct involvement of one or other of these powers. What is really hard to imagine and accept is the possibility of full-scale bloody war with Europe and America as the main antagonists. And the reason why most people would exclude this possibility is the balance of terror; the, probably correct, belief that a war involving nuclear weapons would mean mutual suicide and the more questionable belief that this knowledge has, since the Second World War, deterred the outbreak of another major war. Without exaggerating prophecies of doom, it is important that the last belief be questioned if the possible dangers and follies of the future are to be avoided.

First of all, it can be argued as we have done already that, during the period since the Second World War, neither the United States nor the Soviet Union had any interest in war. Indeed the avoidance of direct confrontation with the West was one of the basic principles underlying Soviet foreign policy. Neither side had anything to gain from war, while both sides profited from the existence of permanent external threat. Victory, defeat or total devastation would have destroyed that threat. The same cannot be said for a future Atlantic conflict. There the threat will be a direct physical threat to the well-being of each side and the conflict will be one which no one wants to perpetuate, in which one side must win and the other lose. According to our argument, each nation can only achieve continued economic expansion at the expense of the other, and expansion is essential to the fabric of Western societies. Failure to expand means not stability but stagnation and decline. It means social frustration in which governments can retain their unenviable position only through increased repression. Precisely because the European and American societies are open systems, with many economic, cultural, and other interconnections between them, any dispute is bound to have much deeper social and political domestic consequences than would a similar dispute between the United States and the Soviet Union. When Europe and America come face to face on an increasing number of issues, it will be much harder to concede for the sake of peace and to avoid actions which might be termed provocative.

A second reason for questioning the belief in the balance of terror is the fact that it is based on agreed strategic concepts and an agreed system of measurement, established by the United States and the Soviet Union – for example, they now talk about strategic 'parity'. This system is not shared by Europe, Japan and China. Nor are these countries likely to adopt it, for it is a system of measurement that emphasizes the superiority of the two current super powers. Yet it is precisely the existence of differing concepts of what constitutes power that leads one or other nation to overestimate its strength and provoke war.[1] The Europeans will, it can be assumed, possess a small nuclear force, based on those currently at the disposal of Britain or France. The high probability that at least one warhead could reach its destination in the event of nuclear attack – from a submarine that wasn't trailed, a hardened silo that escaped destruction, or even from a merchant ship sailing into New York harbour – might encourage the Europeans

---

1. In the First World War, for example, such miscalculations were of considerable importance. In England, as one commentator has pointed out, 'the prediction that the war of 1914 would be short was based heavily on the economic arguments. England was the leading financial power: accordingly, if economic collapse was to come early in the war, it would hit England's enemies first and so lead to their surrender. In contrast German leaders predicted that the war would be short because of the decisiveness of modern military technology; in that field Germany was the recognized master, and so could expect victory.' (Geoffrey Blainey, *The Causes of War*, Macmillan, 1973, p. 40.)

to believe in the credibility of their deterrent. Even if they did not, they might, like North Vietnam, trust to potential allies, armed with nuclear weapons, or to the humane inhibitions against indulging in nuclear warfare. The idea that Europe might learn from Vietnam certain unorthodox approaches to defence, based on local militia and small highly mobile conventional forces, to make up for her assumed inferiority in manpower, money, and advanced weaponry, is already being aired in Europeanist circles. This line of thought might give Europe confidence to embark on provocative international policies.

Equally, however, there is no reason to suppose that the American government should accept such strategic arguments and should not become a victim of its own propaganda. The complicated strategic language, about megatons and mega deaths, may sanctify a belief that America's ability to commit terricide several times over can confer decisive military advantages. While Europeans may take their deterrent and its effects seriously, the Americans regard it as a bit of a joke. The lesson of Vietnam may be forgotten or relegated to the realm of underdeveloped or jungle wars; indeed, this is the more likely, given the endless rehearsal of the Soviet–American drama in the European theatre. In other words, the balance of terror could be upset by America's inability to think beyond the rules of the strategic game established by herself and Russia after the war.

Finally, it should be noted that a bipolar system is more likely to be stable than a multipolar system. In the last two world wars, Germany miscalculated the likelihood of British intervention. With the Soviet Union, China and Japan as potential allies or enemies of Europe and America, with the novelty of international relations, the line between concession and provocation becomes much more nebulous.

This frightening prospect is, of course, predicated upon a European union. The alternative, however, is hardly better. It is, as we have seen, a prolongation of crisis, in which peripheral European governments embark on austerity programmes, under the auspices of American-backed loans, with the use of repression and propaganda to suppress protests. To justify the growth of security forces and the renewed American hegemony, and to isolate those movements offering alternative proposals for change, one can anticipate a resumption of the cold war and a kind of new McCarthyism in which apparently sinister Marxists and Communists are associated, by implication, with Soviet ambitions in Western Europe. This would, of course, be the extreme. One can also anticipate temporary economic recovery in Western Europe, spurred by American loans, perhaps, in which Atlantic preoccupations come to the fore again. The point is that this prospect *is* the prolongation of crisis and that therefore all the alternative prospects – European union or radical social change – remain possible. Indeed, one could argue that ultimately these possibilities must come about unless, that is, the crisis is cut short by new developments in the East–West confrontation which might also entail war.

It has been a major theme in this book that the global struggle between the United States and the Soviet Union has been a kind of necessary ritual, masking real social conflicts that both super powers faced within their own spheres of influence. As mentioned earlier, it was this fact rather than the balance of terror which can be said to explain the absence of a major European war during the last thirty years. Of course, there always was the fairly high risk of accidental war and with the multiplication of strategic systems and computerized forms of control, this risk is escalating. To dwell on this possibility would, however, be a digression. The argument is rather that new dimensions to the relationship between the United States and the Soviet Union, ironically initiated by the process of détente, could undermine the ritual character of their struggle.

The opening up of two closed systems, the new linkages established, could create real conflicts of interest where hitherto none existed. Soviet dependence on Western technology, Soviet indebtedness, the breakdown of the monolithic Soviet bureaucracy in the interests of efficiency and the strains in the Warsaw Pact exacerbated by the introduction of Western ways of doing things, could all create the conditions for the kind of expansionist policy which Western – and Chinese – leaders have predicted in the past. As yet both the interest in and ability for expansion is limited. Indeed, given the Western interest in markets and new sources of raw material and in mutual respect for spheres of influence, there is no reason why Soviet needs should not be fulfilled through an indefinite process of détente. The problem is the dilemma of the West – how to isolate left-wing movements and how to hold the West together without the convenience of an external enemy. (Already, in Italy, Christian Democrats complain that they cannot instil the menace of communism in the minds of Italian voters while Kissinger and Brezhnev hug each other.) The necessary ritual of hostility towards the Soviet Union must involve certain acts, such as the interruption of trade or harsh conditions attached to loans or the isolation of Communist parties in Italy and even Yugoslavia, to be convincing. And it is these acts which could provoke a real expansionary response from the Soviet Union and set off a series of incidents and counter-incidents which could mark the beginning of a lemming-like war.

Is this prospect, like the prospect of an Atlantic war, unduly pessimistic? Surely, Western leaders would come together to prevent war? One must hope that this is so. But one also must be aware of the myopia of governments – the myopia which stems from the absence of political choice, from the knowledge that all course of action involve self-destruction and the gamble that, in uncertain mutual destruction, may be found a solution. People must enter wars short-sightedly; otherwise they would never adopt such insane courses of action. Yet the insanity is only the product of conflict in which there is no sane solution that lies within the current organization of Western society. The leaders of the West owe their existence to this organization; it would be no wonder if they went mad.

Index

AFL–CIO, 20
Acción Democrática, 162
Acheson, Dean, 18
Adenauer, K., 141
Africa, 168–72
  industrialization, 169
  nationalism, 169
  Southern, 170 (*see also* South
    Africa)
  Soviet penetration, 171
  US foreign policy, 171
Agnelli, 167
Aid, 17, 27, 89
Aircraft carriers, 122
Aircraft industry, 51–2, 126–31,
  133–4, 136
Algeria, relations with France,
  156
Alliance for Progress, 163
Alperovitz, Gar, 17
Aluminium: industry, 68 (*see
  also* Bauxite)
  recycling, 108
Amendola, Giorgio, 191

American Popular Revolution-
  ary Alliance (APRA), 162
American Selling Price (ASP),
  96, 99
Andean Group, 165–7
Anderson, Perry, 190
Anglo-Iranian oil company,
  112
Angola, 171
Appeasement, 39
Arab nationalism, 154–7, 160
Aramco, 118
Argentina, 162, 166–8
  arms from France, 164
  military regime, 163
Arms, 35
  bilateral oil deals, 118
  expenditure, 89
  race, control, 30
  see also Defence
Aron, Raymond, 144
Arrighi, Giovanni, 169
Aspin, Les, 26
Aswan Dam, 42

Atlantic Alliance, 18, 94, 141, 145
Atlantic cohesion, 142
Atlanticists, 23, 26
Austria, revaluation, 1971, 85
Autarchy, 45
Automobiles, foundation of US wealth, 59
Aziz, Prince Abdullah Abdul, 157

BASF, 72
Baghdad Pact, 155
Bailey, Richard, 114
Balance of Payments, 70
  correction through devaluation, 75
Balfour declaration, 158
Ball, George, 98, 100
Balmaceda, President, 162
Bank of England, 79
Banking, 91
  commodity speculation, 91
  policies, 45
Baran, 62
Barnet, Richard J., 20, 163
Barraclough, Geoffrey, 12
Basso, Lalio, 188
Bauxite:
  US import dependence, 107
  producer cartels, 108
Bay of Pigs, 163
Bayer, 72
Belgium, 192
Benelux, attitude to European Unity, 192
Bergsten, C. Fred, 90, 97
Berlin, workers uprising, 38
Blainey, Geoffrey, 205
Bölkow, 136
Bolivia, 162
  military regime, 163
Bolshevism, 31-2
Brandt, Willy, 151, 192
Brazil, 162, 164-5
  arms from France, 164
Breguet, see Dassault-Breguet

Bretton Woods, 79-80
British Petroleum (BP), 112-13
Brown, Lester R., 108
Brussels Treaty, 139
Buchan, Alastair, 14
Burrows, Sir Bernard, 144
Business Week, 59, 60, 82-3
Butler, R. A., 187
Butskellism, 187
Butter, 180
Buy American Act, 99
Byrnes, James F., 16

Calleo, David P., 101
Capacity, 34
Capital:
  export, 56
  free movement, 15, 94
Capitalism, 27, 69, 106, 188, 201
  differs from communist system, 31
  liberty as basis, 15
Carrington, Lord, 148-9
Cartels, producer, 108-10
  see also under specific cartels e.g. Organization of Petroleum Exporting Countries (OPEC)
Carter, President, 123, 144
Central Intelligence Agency, 26, 112
Chalfont, Lord, 145
Chemical Industries Association, 75
Chevron, 112
Chile, 162, 164, 168
  coup, 167
Chrysler, 72-3
  Co Com, 43
Coal, 111
Coexistence, 36
  peaceful, 39, 44
Colombia, arms from France, 164
Colonialism, 37, 153

Comecon, 39–40
 trade with USSR, 38
Common Market, 192
 arms policy, 123
 budget, 183
 Common Agricultural Policy
  (CAP), 96, 102–3, 175,
  179–81
 Common External Tariff
  (CXT), 96, 98, 101, 175
 defence integration, 147
 foreign policy, 159
 Kennedy's response, 19
 monetary policies, 84
 1970s enlargement, 25
 relations with Africa, 169–70
 US trade negotiations, 94,
  98
Communism, 25–6, 186–8, 201,
  207
 France, 190
 Italy, 190, 191, 193
 Latin America, 106
Compagnie Française des
  Pétroles, 113
Competitors
 effects on profits, 53
 elimination, 53
Conally, 143
Concentration, 54–5
Confagricoltura, 181
Conference Board, 104
Conflict
 basis of, 47
 domestic, 10
 political, 10
 social, 48
Conseil Intergouvernemental
  de Pays Exporteurs de
  Cuivre (CIPEC), 109
Continental Oil, 113
Cooper, Richard N., 100
Copper, producer cartels, 108
Corporations:
 growth, 48–65
 overseas expansion, 55–65
 state and, 65–77

survival of the fastest, 52–5
 see also Multinational corporations
Council for Mutual Economic
  Assistance (COMECON),
  38–40
Cromwell, William C., 18–19
Cuba, intervention in Angola,
  42
Currencies:
 convertibility, 80
 exchange rates, 72–3, 79–80
 floating, 85, 87
Czechoslovakia, 44, 189

Dahrendorf, Ralf, 181
Dassault, Marcel, 167
Dassault-Breguet, 127, 130–31,
  136
De Chardin, Teilhard, 170
 De Gaulle, Charles, 19, 84,
  141
Debré, M., 144
Declaration of Independence
  (1962), 19, 131
Defence, 122–49, 205–8
 see also Arms
 industry crisis, 125–38
 policy crises, 138–49
 superfluity of Western
  armoury, 31
Denmark, attitude to Euro-
  pean union, 192
Dent, Frederick, 96
Depletion, 107, 110–11
Depreciation, 88–9
Détente, 9–10, 29–30, 41, 43–4,
  85
 Basic Principles, 30, 46
Deutschmark zone, 89
Devaluation, *see* under specific
  countries
Developing countries, *see* Third
  World
Development, uneven, 25, 199
Diebold, William Jnr, 109
Disequilibrium, 105

Dollar:
  convertibility, 84, 86
  overvaluation, 81
  role of, 79, 80
Dominica, 163
Dow Chemical, 72
Du Pont, 72
Dulles, John Foster, 17–18
Dunlop, 72

ENI, 113–14, 159
Ecocide, 12
Ecology, 110
Economic exchange, 30
Economics, connections with
  politics, 48
Economist, 117
Egypt, 42, 155–6
Eisenhower, President, 18
Electronics, 134
Elf/ERAP, 113
Employee/employer inequality,
  69
Enthoven, Alain, 31, 123
Equilibrium, 88
Esso, 73, 112
Euphrates Dam, 42
Eurocurrency, 90
Eurodollars, 83–4, 86–7, 91
Eurogroup, 146
Euromark, 90
Euromoney, 72
Europe, 173–97
  anti-Americanism, 203
  imperialism, 168, 172
  militaristic government, 203
  military integration, 137,
    138, 146, 148, 183
  North–South conflict, 201
  parochialism, 24
  political parties, 184–94
  political union, 183
  relations with Southern
    Africa, 170
  socialist threat, 201
European Coal and Steel Com-
  munity, 19

European Common Market,
  see Common Market
European Council, 184
European Defence Com-
  munity, 140
European Development Fund,
  169
European Economic Com-
  munity, *see* Common
  Market
European Investment Bank,
  169
European Monetary Co-
  operation Fund, 182
European Parliament, 184,
  191
European Programme Group,
  147
European union, 22, 24, 90,
  138, 148, 174, 181–6, 192,
  196, 201–2, 206
Evans, John W., 95
Exchange rates, *see* Currencies:
  exchange rates
Experience curve, 50
Exports
  ab initio agreements, 73
  economic growth through,
    56
  effects of exchange rates, 73
Exxon, 112, 118

Fabrique Nationale, 127
Faisal, King of Saudi Arabia,
  116
Fascism, 154
Federal Reserve, 80, 82, 91
Fiscal policy, 72
Fisher, Fritz, 23
Fleming, Denna Frank, 17
Flores, Paolo, 194
Fokker, 127
Food
  scarcity, 12
  world prices, 21
Ford, President, 125, 141
Forrestal, James V., 18

France
  army unrest, 194–5, 200
  attitude to European union,
    192
  autonomist movements, 193
  communism, 45, 190
  devaluation, 178
  exports to Arab countries,
    158
  left alliance, 191, 193
  mergers, 55
  political threat, 199
  preference for gold, 86
  relations with Latin America,
    164
  relations with Middle East,
    156
  Soviet Treaty of Friendship,
    43
Frank, André Gunder, 162
Franklin National Bank, 91
Free trade, 94, 97, 100, 106
Frei, President, 164
Frobenius, Leo, 170

Gaitskell, Hugh, 187
Galbraith, J. K., 31
Gardner, C. Lloyd, 16
Garibaldi, G., 23
Gaullism, 19, 23–4, 186,
    193
Geiger, Theodore, 196–7
General Agreement on Tariffs
    and Trade (GATT), 40,
    95–8, 100, 103
General Motors, 73
General Signal Corp., 60
Generalized preference, 100,
    101
Germany, West;
  attitude to European union,
    192
  European domination, 203
  exports, 89
  mark floated (1971), 85
  rearmament, 18
  revaluation (1969), 84

Soviet Treaty of Friendship,
    43
Getulism, 162
Ghana, 169
Giscard d'Estaing, V., 87, 183
Godson, Joseph, 142
Gold standard, 79, 81, 86
Goldman, Marshall I., 45
Goldsborough, James R., 144,
    146, 151
Goulart, President, 164
Government, internal organ-
    ization, 66
Gramscian notion, 190
Gromyko A. A., 39
'Group of 77', 152
Growth, 31, 34, 55
Gulf Oil, 112

Harman, Chris, 38
Heath, Edward, 146, 150
Helsinki Conference, 39
Helwan steel complex, 42
Heyhoe, D. C. R., 147
Holland, Stuart, 71
Horowitz, D., 17, 25, 38
Howard Johnson, 54
Hull, Cordell, 94
Humphrey, Hubert, 102
Hungary
  revolution (1956), 38
  Soviet influence on trade
    agreements, 40
Huntingdon, Samuel, 123
Hymer, 56

Imperialism, 11, 76, 168, 172
Imports
  effects of exchange rates, 73
  US restrictions, 22
India, Soviet stake, 42
Industrialization, 33, 35, 153,
    154, 162, 169
Inflation, 178
  depreciation effects, 88
  erosion of benefits of
    devaluation, 73

Inflation—*cont.*
  recession with, 75
Innovation, 49–52, 59, 60, 177
Institute of Economic Affairs,
  120
Inter-American Development
  Bank, 166
Interest rates, 72
International Business
  Machines (IBM), 49–50
International Harvester, 74
International Monetary Fund,
  45, 79–80, 86
Intervention, military, 27, 41
Investment, 49–52, 60, 177
Iran, 159–60
  relations with Arab
    countries, 160
Iran, Shah of, 112
Iraq:
  relations with France, 156,
    158
  relations with Iran, 160
  relations with Soviets, 42,
    155
Ireland, attitude to European
  union, 192
Iron ore, US import depend-
  ence, 107
Irwin, Christopher, 144
Italy, 176–7
  attitude to European union,
    192
  communism, 45, 190–91, 193
  devaluation, 178
  political threat, 199

Jackson-Nunn amendment,
  142
Jalée, Pierre, 11
Jantsch, Erich, 59
Japan, oil policy, 114
Jequier, Nicholas, 49, 50
Jiménez, Pérez, 112
Jobert, Michel, 119, 122–3,
  146, 151
Johnson, Lyndon, 15

Kaiser, Karl, 145
Kennan, George, 9, 18
Kennedy, John F., 19, 94–6,
  131, 163
Kennedy Round, 95
Khrushchev, N., 39, 189
Kidron, Michael, 42
Kissinger, Henry, 25–6, 29,
  118–19, 143–4, 150–51, 172
Kogan, Norman, 188
Koser, Michael, 39
Kosygin, A. N., 39
Kondratieff, 58
Kuwait:
  attitude to Israel, 157
  relations with France, 158

Labini, Sylos, 50, 75
Labour, free movement, 94
Lafeber, Walter, 17, 84, 139
Laissez-faire, 65
Land reform, 153
Lanusse, President, 164
Latin America, 161–8
  arms deals, 164
  communism, 166
  industrialization, 162
  nationalism, 161–3, 168
  US aid, 163
Latin American Free Trade
  Area (LAFTA), 165
Lenin, V. I., 32, 33, 190
Levinson, Charles, 75
Liberalism, 10, 15, 186, 187
Liberia, 169
Liberty, 31
Libya:
  attitude to Israel, 157
  nationalism, 156
  relations with France, 158
Lockheed, 66–7, 131
Lomé Convention, 169
Lotharingia, 20, 23–4, 27, 174,
  178, 192, 196, 201
Luns, Joseph, 147

MFN, 100

MLF, 131
MPLA, 171
McCarthyism, 207
McNamara, 19, 123
Magdoff, Harry, 11, 143
Malenkov, G. M., 38–9
Mandel, Ernest, 11
Mansfield amendment, 142
Mansfield resolution, 145
Marathon Oil, 113
Marcuse, Herbert, 33–4, 37
Market, the, 49–52, 60
Market expansion, 53
Market-sharing, 73–4
Marshall Aid, 17, 45, 139, 202
Marxism, 10, 31, 186, 190, 194, 207
Massey-Ferguson, 40, 74
Materials:
    scarcity panics, 107
    see also Supplies
Mattei, 159
Mazzini, G., 23, 186
Medvedev, Roy, 36
Meier, Gerald, 95
Melman, Seymour, 64
Mergers, 54–5
Messerschmitt-Bölkow-Blohm, 137
Michelin, 72
Middle East, 154–62
    crisis, October 1973, 150–51
Missiles, 32, 122
Mitsui, 74
Mitterand, François, 194, 200
Mobil, 112, 114, 118
Monetary policy, 71
Money, 78–92
Monopoly, profits, 50
Montedison, 72
Moretti, Franco, 194
Müller, Ronald E., 20, 163
Multi Role Combat Aircraft (MRCA), 133, 136
Multinationals, 11, 20, 22, 24, 62

effects on currencies, 82–3
effects on trade, 83, 178
pricing, 178
rise of, 70
see also Corporations
Multipolarity, 12
Murray, Robin, 71
Mussadeq, Dr, 112

NIOC, 113
Nation state:
    definition, 10
    super, 12
National Revolutionary Movement (MNR), 162
National specialization, 136
Nationalism, *see* under specific countries/areas
Nationalization, 153
Nenni, Pietro, 188
Netherlands, guilder floated (1971), 85
New Dealers, 16–17, 23, 94
New Economic Policy, 85
New Mercantilism, 23
Newbould, Gerald, 55
Niedergang, Marcel, 162–3
Nixon, President, 12, 31, 85–6, 102, 111, 119, 151
Nixon Round, 97
Nkrumah, K., 169
North Atlantic Treaty, 139
North Atlantic Treaty Organization (NATO), 18, 22, 26, 123–4, 135, 138–49, 159, 200, 202
Nuclear:
    deterrent, 145
    energy, 111
    parity, 141

OGIL, 190
O'Connor, James, 70
O'Kane, Bernard, 134
Odell, Prof. Peter, 110
Oil, 106–21

Oil—*cont.*
　Arab embargo, 90, 110, 117,
　　120, 157, 159
　bilateral arms deals, 118
Oligopology, 54
Oliver, Covey, 163
Olivetti, 72
Organization of African Unity
　(OAU), 169, 170
Organization of Petroleum
　Exporting Countries
　(OPEC), 101, 115, 117
Orwell, George, 12

Pachachi, Nadim, 116
Pan Africanism, 169
Panavia, 136–7
Parities, *see* Currencies:
　exchange rates
Parliament, sovereignty, 192
Parochialism:
　Europe, 24
　USA, 20–22, 26–7, 43–5,
　　140, 147, 196
Patolichev, Nikolai S., 43
Perón, Pres., 167
Peronism, 162
Perroux, R., 20
Peru, 161, 166, 167
　military regime, 163
Peterson, Peter G., 104
Petrofina, 113
Petromin, 113
Philips, 73
Phillips Petroleum, 113
Pisar, Samuel, 36, 39
Pius XII, Pope, 185
Planning, 31, 35
Poland, revolution (1956), 38
Politics, connections with
　economics, 48
Pollack, George A., 90
Polycentrism, 44, 189
Pompidou, President, 84, 186
Powellites, 186
Power, concepts, 205
Prediction, 197

Price-fixing, 73, 178
Procter and Gamble, 60
Production, cost of, 53
Productivity, 34–5, 63–4
Profitability, criteria for, 57
Profits:
　effects of competition, 53–4
　monopoly, 50
Project Independence, 111
Protection, 97, 107, 179
Public spending, real nature, 69

Radice, Hugo, 11
Raw materials, *see* Materials:
　supplies
Raytheon, 125
Recession, with inflation, 75
Recycling, 108
Renault, 72, 164
Research and development, 60
Restrepo, Lleras. 165
Rhodesia, 170
Richardson, Keith, 115
Rinascita, 188
Robots, 51
Rockefeller, David, 39
Rockwell International, 66
Rolls-Royce, 131, 136
Romania, reparations, 38
Roosevelt, F. D., 16
Rosenthal, Bert, 163
Rothschild, Emma, 21, 49, 59,
　72
Rowland, Benjamin M., 101
Rowthorn, R., 11, 56
Royal Dutch Shell, 112–13
Rumsfield, D. H., 122

SABCA, 127
SKF, 73
SNECMA, 131
St Gobain, 72
Sakharov, A. D., 36
Saudi Arabia, 157
　Aramco, 118
　relations with France, 158
　relations with US, 160

Saul, John S., 169
Schlesinger, James, 141
Schmidt, Helmut, 104, 152
Schmoller, Gustav, 23
Schumpeter, 58, 59
Servan-Schreiber, J-J., 61
Scientific exchange, 30
Senegal, 170
Senghor, President Leopold, 170
Shale rock, 111
Shell, *see* Royal Dutch Shell
Shipbuilding, 128–9
Shultz, 106
Singer, 72
Smith, Wayne, 31, 123
Smithsonian Institute, 85
SoCal, 112, 118
Social harmony, 69–70
Socialism, 154
Society of British Aerospace Companies, 130
Solvay, 72
Sonatrach, 113
Sonnenfeldt, Helmut, 30
South Africa, 170–71
Sovereignty, 78, 192
Soviets:
  African penetration, 171
  aid, 42
  arms build-up, 32
  colonization, 37
  differences with capitalist system, 31
  economic integration, 44
  economic reforms (1960s), 36
  expansion, 207–8
  foreign policy, 204
  hegemony, 191
  military spending, 26, 123
  need for Western technology, 34, 37, 44, 207
  relations with US, 207
  reparations, 38, 43
  Third World policies, 43
  trade with Comecon, 38
  trade with US, 43

  trade with West, 39–40, 43–4
  Treaties of Friendship, 43, 136
Soya, 103
Spain, 69
Speculation, 82, 83, 87
  by banks, 91
  stabilization effects, 88
Special Drawing Rights (SDRs), 80, 86, 87, 201
Spinelli, Altiero, 173
Stalin, J., 33, 37, 189
Standard Oil of California, 112
Standard Oil of Indiana, 113
Standard Oil of New Jersey, 112
Standard Oil of New York, 112
State, functions of, 67–8
Sterling, 79
Stockpiles, 108
Strategic Arms Limitation Talks (SALT), 145
Strauss, F.-J., 146
Submarines, 32, 122
Sun Oil, 113
Sunbeam, 72
Sunday Times, 115
Supplies:
  access to, 106, 107
  security of, 113
  see also Materials
Supply mercantilism, 107
Supreme Allied Command Europe (SACEUR), 139
Sutton, Antony C., 34
Sweezy, 62, 143
Switzerland, revaluation (1971), 85
Sykes–Picot agreement, 158
Syria:
  relations with China, 156
  relations with Soviets, 155
  relations with US, 42, 156

Tanzania, military *coup*, 169
Tar sands, 111

Tariffs, 15, 40, 95, 97–8; *see also* General Agreement on Tariffs and Trade
Taxation, 72
Tensions, understanding, 10
Texaco, 112, 118
Third World, 150–72, 202
  generalized preferences, 100
  military intervention, 41
  Soviet penetration, 42
Ticktin, H., 35
Tin, US import dependence, 107
Togliatti, Palmiro, 188–9
Tokyo Declaration, 98
Toyota, 51
Trade Act (1975), 107
Trade Bill (1973), 102
Trade Expansion Act (1962), 19, 94
Trade Reform Act (1973), 97
Trentin, Bruno, 190
Trotskyites, 31
Truman, President, 17, 38
Tugendhat, Christopher, 61
Turchin, 36
Two-Way Street, 135, 137, 138, 147

UNCTAD, 101
Union de la Gauche Socialiste et Démocrate, 191, 193
Union of Soviet Socialist Republics (USSR), *see* Soviets
Unions, 195
United Kingdom:
  attitude to European union, 192
  Common Market entry vetoed, 19
  devaluation, 178
  Labour government, 195
  mergers, 55
  nationalism, 193
  nineteenth-century role, 16
  political threat, 199

United Shoe, 74
United States of America:
  aid to Latin America, 163
  European defence spending, 142
  European resentment, 132
  export of domestic problems, 76
  foreign investment in, 89
  foreign policy, 16, 21–2
  in Africa, 171
  hegemony, 11, 92, 148, 172, 191, 197, 203, 207
  import restrictions, 97
  internationalism, 160
  mergers, 54
  parochialism, 20–22, 26–7, 43–5, 140, 147, 196
  raw material imports, 107
  relations with Common Market, 94, 98, 159
  relations with Middle East, 156–7
  relations with Saudi Arabia, 160
  relations with Soviets, 43, 207
  reversal of growth position, 20
  role as central banker, 82
  substitution of imperialism for inflation, 76
  trade deficit, 21
  Vietnam involvement, 85
  world corporate expansion effects, 76
United States Arms Control and Disarmament Agency, 144
United States Export-Import Bank, 109
United States National Commission of Materials Policy, 109
US Rubber, 72
Unity, halting communism, 25
Ursus, 40

Ustinov, 36

VFW, 127
Value Added Tax, 99
Values, changes, 48
Varga (Soviet economist), 11
Vargas, Getulio, President of
    Brazil, 162
Venezuela, 162, 164
Vernon, R., 49
Vietnam, 85
    consequence in US, 14
    lessons of, 206
War:
    avoidance, 36–7, 41, 44, 204
    causes, 204
    cold, 10, 45, 126
    nuclear, 205
Warnke, Paul C., 144

Warsaw Pact, 44, 124, 208
Western European Union
    (WEU), 140, 151; *see also*
    European union
Williams, William Appleman,
    16, 17
Williams Report, 102
Willis, F. Roy, 18–19, 188
Wilson, Woodrow, 15
Wine, 180
Woolworth, 53

Yamani, Sheikh, 115
Yaounde Convention, 169

Zambia, military coup, 169
Zhdanov, 37
Ziegler, Henri, 133
Zinoviev, G. E., 33

More About Penguins and Pelicans

I HAVEN'T HAD TO GO MAD HERE
Joseph H. Berke

When someone is labelled as 'mentally ill', he is deprived of his autonomy and stifled with drugs, E C T or psychosurgery – mainly, argues the author, for the benefit of society and the medical profession. The patient, meanwhile, retreats into an immobilizing dependence from which he may never emerge.

This book describes Joseph Berke's experiences at his Arbours Centre, where psychosis and distress are regarded as important human experiences to be accepted, lived through and shared, not condemned; where patients are given 'the space, the time and the encouragement to do, to be and to become more than they have previously been allowed'.

TOYS AND PLAYTHINGS
John and Elizabeth Newson

John and Elizabeth Newson need no introduction as one of the most distinguished and influential research teams in child development and early behaviour. This fascinating, detailed, sometimes nostalgic analysis of hundreds of toys and their varied roles in children's development includes also important sections on 'Using Toys and Play Remedially' and 'Toys and Play for the Sick Child'.

AFRICA UNDERMINED
Mining Companies and the Underdevelopment of Africa
Greg Lanning with Marti Mueller

This is a uniquely informative critical history of the relationship between the mining companies and the development of Africa. It is a story of colonization and colonialism; of ruthless greed and irresponsible exploitation; of self-interest protected and profit pursued.

Greg Lanning and Marti Mueller show how this plunder has undermined and distorted Africa's internal physical, political and economic structures and her international status. 'From the start,' they argue, 'the companies have constantly supported the white minority, and exploited the black majority. Only history can tell how that majority will react to the companies when majority rule finally arrives'.

POWER POLITICS
Martin Wight

Concentrating not on the ephemera of current events but on the features of international politics that are fundamental and enduring, Martin Wight has written a classical account of the international system that arose in Europe at the beginning of modern times, spread itself over other continents, and still provides the framework of the world.

Notable for its clarity, balance, judgement and formidable erudition, *Power Politics* is a definitive contribution to the study of politics.

VIABLE DEMOCRACY
Michael Margolis

Professor Margolis describes his project in these words: 'We must build up a theory of viable democracy, one that preserves traditional concerns for individual self development through political participation, but one that also takes into account the realities of the bureaucracy, the military and corporate establishment, and the environment'. If democracy is to resist onslaughts from both right and left, major reforms are essential. *Viable Democracy* both recognizes this and offers a challenging possibility for the future.

IRAN: DICTATORSHIP AND DEVELOPMENT
Fred Halliday

Fred Halliday, whose punchy, informative and critical book constitutes a timely addition to the debate on Iran's future, proffers some surprising conclusions on the subject. Bringing together for the first time social, political and economic factors, he gives the layman a rigorous and readable analysis of this harsh and divided country – the State today, its historical origins, its economic policies and instruments of repression, its opposition and the future of the present régime.

One thing, says the author is certain: 'If Iran remains in political and cultural terms anything like what it was in the 1970s then it will remain a brutal, philistine society, marked be extreme inequalities. Such a society will have nothing great and little civilized about it'.